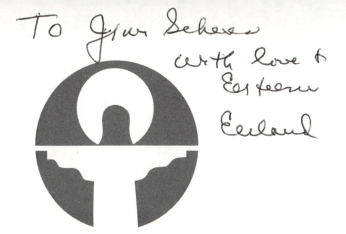

JESUS CHRIST

AND THE MISSION

OF THE CHURCH

Contemporary Anabaptist Perspectives

Faith and Life Press
Newton, Kan

D0024400

Printed in the United States of America

93 92 91 90 4 3 2 1

Library of Congress Number 90-82027

International Standard Book Number 0-87303-138-5

Editorial
direction for Faith and Life Press by Maynard Shelly, general editor; copy editing by Edna Dyck and Delia Graber;
design by John Hiebert; printing by Mennonite Press.

The publishers gratefully acknowledge the assistance of
the Schowalter Foundation in the publication of this book.

Foreword

Since the children of the Anabaptists commonly speak of theirs as a Christ-centered faith, identity and mission become two focal issues facing Mennonite and Brethren in Christ people today. Christian identity, more than we may think, hinges on how we answer the classic question of Jesus, "Who do you say that I am?" Since Christian mission will issue directly out of Christian identity, these two foci of ecclesiastical and missiological discussion are inextricably related.

This publication emerged out of dialogue among Mennonite and Brethren in Christ mission agencies consulting in the context of the Eleventh Mennonite World Conference in Strasbourg, France, in 1984. The Council of Moderators and Secretaries, representing the Mennonite Church, the General Conference Mennonite Church, the Mennonite Brethren Church, and the Brethren in Christ, took seriously the call to bring together a study conference on Christology and its missionary implications, on August 4-6, 1989, at Illinois State University, Normal, Illinois.

The purpose of this study conference was for representatives of these church bodies to "enter into serious dialogue concerning our understanding of the person, the work, and the ethical and missiological significance of Jesus Christ in the life and ministry of our people, to clarify our faith positions, to identify areas of commonality and differences, and to promote better mutual understanding and greater unity among our groups as we together witness that *Jesus Christ is Lord.*"

The study conference began with the preparation and

publication of four major study papers which were distributed to over seven hundred conferees who registered to attend. Because interest in this theme exceeded the capacity for participation in the study conference sessions at Normal, Illinois, it was decided to republish these papers together with two of the prepared responses (by Daniel D. García Swartzentruber and Mary H. Schertz) and the report of the Findings Committee. Some minor revisions in the original papers have also been included, as well as a response to the J. Denny Weaver paper by Thomas Finger.

This publication is now released with the understanding that the papers represent in substance and style the authors themselves and do not constitute any kind of common consensus on the part of the program planners nor of the various conferences or institutions the authors may be serving. The individual writers are themselves accountable for the positions espoused and articulated. Deep appreciation, however, is expressed to these writers for initiating these important discussions among Mennonites and Brethren in Christ.

Readers should bear in mind that the authors were urged to remember that they would be communicating with congregational leaders rather than the scholars of the church or their respective professional guilds. The study process is perceived as continuing beyond the study conference itself. This is reflected in the report of the Findings Committee which is also published in this volume.

The planning committee for the Study Conference on Christology included James Lapp, Elkhart, Indiana (Mennonite Church); Vern Preheim, Newton, Kansas (General Conference Mennonite Church); Herbert Brandt, Kelowna, British Columbia (Mennonite Brethren Church); and Don Shafer, Upland, California (Brethren in Christ).

In addition to the four basic papers, written by George Brunk III, Harrisonburg, Virginia; John E. Toews, Fresno, California; Harry Huebner, Winnipeg, Manitoba; and J. Denny Weaver, Bluffton, Ohio, the conference included thirteen focus group sessions with topics and leaders as follows:

Believers Church Christology in Historical Perspective; J. Denny Weaver, Bluffton, Ohio.

Christologies in the Four Gospels: Implications for Missions; Dorothy Jean Weaver, Harrisonburg, Virginia.

Jesus in Trinitarianism; A. James Reimer, Waterloo, Ontario.

The Centrality of Jesus Christ in Evangelistic Proclamation; Myron Augsburger, Washington, D. C.

Christology in Missionary Context; Wilbert Shenk, Elkhart, Indiana.

The Human and Divine Character of Jesus Christ; E. Morris Sider, Grantham, Pennsylvania.

The Importance of Experience versus the Doctrine of Christ; Luke L. Keefer, Jr., Ashland, Ohio.

Various Views of the Atonement; Jerry Ediger, Winnipeg.

Jesus and Creation; Patricia Shelly, North Newton, Kansas.

Christology and Liberation Theologies; Daniel Schipani, Elkhart, Indiana.

Christology and Feminism; Rachel Helen Reesor, Montreal.

Is Christ Normative for Knowing God? Thomas Finger, Harrisonburg, Virginia.

Christology and Historical Objectivity; Ted Grimsrud, Eugene, Oregon.

The members of the Findings Committee were Marlin E. Miller (Mennonite Church), chair; John Arthur Brubaker (Brethren in Christ); Tim Geddert (Mennonite Brethren Church); Lydia Harder (General Conference Mennonite Church); Elmer Jantzi (Conservative Mennonite Conference); and Robert J. Suderman (missionary, General Conference Mennonite Church).

Faith and Life Press and Maynard Shelly, as its general editor, assisted with the publication of this book. All who have served us in any way in this endeavor are sincerely thanked. May God be pleased to bless this publishing venture for use in congregations and in educational institutions as well as for individual study.

ERLAND WALTNER, Elkhart, Indiana
Editor and Coordinator of Study Conference Planning

v

Contents

The exclusiveness of Jesus Christ

George Brunk III

Many sectors of contemporary Christendom are experiencing a "Christological failure of nerve."[1] Convictions regarding the significance of Jesus Christ for the human experience are wavering; actions aimed at mediating Jesus Christ to the human race are weakening. This is the loss of nerve.

On the other hand, in our time as in the past, there are those of a fanatical mind-set who confuse their limited human cause with the final cause of God and his Christ.[2] Interestingly, those who choose either one of these extremes often appear to do so as an escape from the evils of the opposite extreme. This vacillation between a loss of nerve and a spirit of presumption illustrates the central problem in the question of the exclusiveness of Jesus Christ, especially as that question bears upon the mission of the church. Is there an alternative to these opposites that both answers to the claims of the Christian message and provides a viable style of mission activity?

1. This helpful expression was used in the pluralistic context of the Association of Theological Schools in a statement on globalization presented at its 1988 biennial meeting and therefore has the force of a confession, not a condemnation.

2. It has become common practice to use the term *fundamentalist* to describe movements of this kind, both of Christian and other religious orientation. This is unfortunate. In its plain meaning, this term describes one with convictions about certain foundational truths held to be indispensable. Its usage in this pejorative sense only reinforces the perception of our age that intolerance is the inevitable result of holding convictions.

What exactly do we mean by the exclusiveness of Jesus Christ? We mean that which marks the person of Jesus Christ as singular and unique so as to make of him an unparalleled and unsurpassable means of salvation. Parallel expressions are the finality or the supremacy of Jesus Christ. Yet another phrase with a similar concern is "the absoluteness of Christianity."[3] However, posing the question in relation to Christianity is, as we will see, not the same as posing it in relation to Jesus Christ. Christianity, in the sense of the historical manifestation of Christian belief, is not the same as the historical manifestation of truth in the person of Jesus Christ. The various modes of expression have their strengths and shortcomings. It is not the present purpose to decide on the relative merits of the language. We will use a variety of terms.

While the term *exclusiveness* has a long history, it has a negative ring in our inclusive age. Perhaps this is helpful in the end for it helps sharpen the issues for us. In all events, when used in relation to Jesus Christ, the term does not carry the common connotation of shutting out another or disassociation from others. However the uniqueness of Jesus Christ is to be construed, no one will contest the fact that this uniqueness coexists with and, indeed, supplies the ground for a universal significance of this person. Here exclusiveness and inclusiveness commingle.

To further develop our theme, we will first consider the current cultural context that conditions our question. Then attention will be given to the scriptural evidence as it bears on the subject. Finally, the focus will be on the implications of a right understanding of Christ's claim for the missionary practice of the church.

The present state of the question

It has practically become a truism to describe our times as

3. The former language is illustrated by the recent book by Stephen Neill, *The Supremacy of Jesus* (Downers Grove: Intervarsity, 1984). The latter terminology was given prominence by Ernst Troeltsch early in the century. His writing is available in English translation as *The Absoluteness of Christianity and the History of Religion* (Richmond: John Knox, 1971). Troeltsch embraces a relativistic position; Neill defends the uniqueness of Jesus.

relativistic. Allen Bloom in his best-selling book, *The Closing of the American Mind*, aptly expresses our situation by what he sees among university students:

> They are unified only in their relativism and in their allegiance to equality. . . . The relativity of truth is not a theoretical insight but a moral postulate, the condition of a free society, or so they see it. . . . The danger they have been taught to fear from absolutism is not error but intolerance. Relativism is necessary to openness; and this is the virtue, the only virtue, which all primary education for more than fifty years has dedicated itself to inculcating. Openness—and the relativism that makes it the only plausible stance in the face of various claims to truth and various ways of life and kinds of human beings—is the great insight of our times. The true believer is the real danger (pp. 25-26).

What is here attributed to the mind-set of the student generation is equally true of Western society as a whole. Tolerance is the great virtue and a relative understanding of truth is its corollary. Pluralism is both a cause and effect of this outlook. Perhaps its deeper root is the autonomous reason of the Enlightenment which, once set free from any authority, fragments into a multiplicity of viewpoints and finally loses all confidence in itself. Pluralism and relativism are the products.

The point for the present discussion is simply this: if tolerance is the sole virtue, then exclusiveness becomes the vice. Whether tolerance and exclusive claims to truth are necessarily incompatible is not the point here. Our society, given its understanding of tolerance based in relativism, finds the question of exclusiveness to be a stumbling block and a scandal. We can harbor no illusion about the status of our interest in the exclusiveness of Jesus Christ. The matter will be coolly rejected or hotly resisted.

It was noted that relativism and pluralism are mutually related. The relativism from the Western enlightenment has contributed to the breakdown of uniform beliefs in society. On the other hand, pluralism has its own long history of diverse religions and worldviews among peoples. Within Christianity, Anabaptism itself has been a major contributor to the rise of pluralism in the West with its commitment to voluntarism in faith and a church free from politi-

3

cal control. Pluralism antedates relativism and has helped to create it.

Developments in the modern world bring us increasingly in contact with the pluralism of religious beliefs. Faraway places have come closer by new means of travel and communication; the faraway peoples have come nearer by massive migration to new cultural and religious contexts. Alternate visions of life become part of our daily experience and the questions of coexistence with them are unavoidable. One writer concludes that "The new perception of religious pluralism is pushing our cultural consciousness toward the simple but profound insight that *there is no one and only way.*"[4] Here it is not a question of whether this perception is correct or not. We simply recognize that the pluralistic context of our times places increasing pressure on the claim of exclusiveness of all faiths, including Christianity.

While pluralism has long been present in the human experience, it was looked upon as abnormal, reflecting the limitations of human understanding or the moral failure of the human family. Today many are inclined to search for a way to accommodate to pluralism, to normalize it by acknowledging that reality is fundamentally plural in nature. This is tersely expressed in the statement: "Today, the universe of meaning has no center."[5]

Those with this outlook are not arguing for a pure relativism of truth nor for a fixing of the diversity of religious faiths. Rather they are attracted to the general outlook of process philosophy for making sense of pluralism. According to this outlook, the world is in the process of becoming. What we experience now is pluralism, but the process is leading toward unity. In this vision, all aspects of present reality are seen as significant for each aspect contributes to the movement toward convergence. The shape of that convergence is by definition unknown, although Christian thinkers with this perspective may characterize that future

4. Paul Knitter, *No Other Name?* (Maryknoll: Orbis Books, 1985), p. 5. The following discussion on pluralism is indebted to Knitter.

5. Nicholas Lash, *Theology on Dover Beach* (New York: Paulist, 1979), p. 71.

in the light of past revelation.[6] Along with the key concept of *becoming* is an emphasis on *interrelating*. The process of becoming takes place in the interrelating of all aspects of reality. Relationship defines being, not the other way around. This principle holds true for the realm of human experience as in other realms. The emphasis on interrelating carries into the religious arena since the search for truth occurs in the interaction between religions.

When one takes this approach to understanding reality, many of the Christian beliefs must be either rejected or reinterpreted. For example, the doctrines of Creation and the Fall have said that the universe began with a unity in the act of creation but lost that unity by reason of sin and its fragmenting consequences. This requires that the plurality of truth claims in history have to be weighed in the light of both a principle of coherence with the beginning norm and a principle of morality. In other words, the question of right or wrong has to be addressed to the diverse claimants of truth. The radical affirmation of pluralism, however, appears to renounce any ground or right to pass such judgment since truth is in the becoming process.

In the preceding paragraphs, we have explored two important tendencies of our social context—relativism and pluralism. The purpose has been evocative rather than exhaustive. The intention is to illustrate why and how the exclusiveness of Jesus Christ is a problem in our time. A critique of this contemporary viewpoint is not our primary interest. What is of significance is the recognition that we are not immune to the formative impact of these issues.

The spirit of the age has taken root and bears its fruit in our souls, perhaps more than we realize. We, as followers of Christ, are conditioned to stumble at his claim. All of this does not yet answer the question of how we are to understand the question of the exclusiveness of Jesus Christ. It does, however, alert us that the temptation we face is not only to be driven by self-interest and will-to-power under the guise of exclusive claims for our religion, but also to sell out the exclusive claim of Another under

6. The most notable of Christian attempts with this approach is that of Teilhard de Chardin

the pretense of acknowledging the relativity of our own knowledge and achievements.

The claims of Scripture
for the exclusiveness of Jesus Christ

The evidence of Scripture suggests that the question before us does not yield to a simple, unilateral answer. It is not a matter of the New Testament sounding an uncertain note about Christ's absolute significance for all people. Friend and foe alike tend to agree that, when taken on its own terms, the New Testament does make exclusive claims for Jesus the Christ. However, in the biblical writing, there is no systematic and full defense of these claims as a theoretical problem over against other religions. In fact, the biblical writers are reserved about speculation concerning the present status or the future destiny of individual nonbelievers. They are profoundly interested, however, in the moral condition of humanity and its relation to the future destiny of humankind. They are deeply committed to share the gospel with all persons in the belief that Christ offers something to everyone. But there is a disinterest or reticence to draw a precise line between truth and nontruth, between salvation and damnation, *in their historical expression.*[7]

A clue to this status of the question is found already on the lips of Jesus himself. On one occasion, the disciple John informed Jesus that a certain man was casting out demons in Jesus' name but was not ready to follow him. To this Jesus responded, "He who is not against us is for us" (Mark 9:38-40, RSV). However, on another occasion, when Jesus defended his deliverance ministry as a conflict of God's kingdom with the kingdom of Satan, he made a parallel but reverse assertion: "He who is not with me is against me; and he who does not gather with me scatters" (Luke 11:23).

7. These statements are open to misunderstanding. They do not mean that the Bible expresses uncertainty about its claims or indifference about the moral and spiritual consequences of human action. There is even a readiness to pass judgment on clear cases of right and wrong, truth and error. Still, we need to recognize that biblical writers do not pretend to know where the precise line of God's saving pronouncement falls for individuals and peoples.

It seems apparent that for Jesus the question of his own exclusive claim cannot be answered in the same way in relation to every other claimant of truth. In the second instance, Jesus sets himself clearly in exclusive contrast to the kingdom of evil. This is not surprising. The world is the arena for the clash of good and evil. All must, and, in fact, inevitably do, take sides on the issue. In the other account, there is a religious leader who, while using Jesus' name, does not identify with the same program and community of Jesus and his immediate disciples. Jesus includes him without demanding that he participate in his own social circle. The movement of Jesus is bigger than the historical structures which are organically related to him.

But the story does not answer our question definitively. Since the independent exorcist uses the name of Jesus, there is a link to the messianic claim of Jesus. This is not just any religionist. We do not have here, for instance, the grounds for affirming that the movement of God is larger than the messianic movement of Jesus. The case falls within the classical formulation in Acts 4:12: "no other name. . . by which we must be saved." We are, however, put on notice that error lurks on more than one side of the question of Jesus' exclusive claim and its bearing on the practice of mission by the church. In the expression, "he who is not against us is for us," there is disclosed both a clear sense of a cause promoted by an identifiable movement (us) and a recognition that this cause, the cause of God, is not dependent exclusively upon that one movement. The necessary implication is that the nature of this cause is one that can be related to and supported in unexpected ways, perhaps even unwittingly.

The claim of Jesus

The search turns then toward the wider evidence of the New Testament to confirm and to clarify the kind of perspective seen in the above sayings of Jesus. There are, of course, the well-known standard passages to which appeal is rightly made. "I am the way, and the truth, and the life; no one comes to the Father, but by me" (John 14:6). "There is salvation in no one else, for there is no other name" by which persons must be saved (Acts 4:12). "For there is one God, and there is one mediator between God and men, the man Christ Jesus" (1 Tim. 2:5). The book of Hebrews sounds a strong exclusivist note with the definition of Christ's work as "once for all" (9:12).

While no one is prepared to argue that the early Christians intended anything other than implied by this exclusive language, there are some who wish to reinterpret its meaning for today. They may argue that the worldview of the first Christians with its static view of truth and God-determined, end-oriented view of history, and upon which the language of Christ's finality is based, is no longer tenable. Moreover, this language is said to express the believers' confidence in their faith experience, rather than to formulate with precision the relationship of Jesus Christ to all other claims of salvation.[8]

In order to attempt some weighing of these matters for ourselves, we should look again at the fundamental reality of New Testament beliefs as rooted in the life and teaching of Jesus. As careful biblical students know, it was not the practice of Jesus to center his message in himself directly nor to make explicit claims about his person.[9] Nothing illustrates this more strikingly than Jesus' use of the self designation of "son of man." This enigmatic expression, with its potential meanings of either the most human or most transcendent, divine dimensions, was puzzling both then as now. It is as if Jesus' self descriptions are to his person what his use of parables was to his teaching—they helped those inclined to perceive, but caused those inclined to unbelief to misunderstand. (See Mark 4:11,12.) This may well explain also why Jesus avoided the messianic

8. So for example, Knitter, *No Other Name*, pp. 182-86.
9. Some readers will wonder how this relates to the Gospel of John where Jesus (and the writer) are more direct, as in John 14:6 quoted earlier. The synoptic Gospels no doubt reflect more of the feel of Jesus' lifetime. John's Gospel teaches that the disciples understood Jesus' life *after his exaltation* in a better way by the Spirit's leading (2:22, *et al*). The Gospel appears to be written in the light of the latter, fuller understanding. To what extent this fuller perspective is placed in Jesus' mouth or Jesus' statements are special recollections of John that the synoptic writers did not have is impossible to say. Either way should be no problem for a belief in inspiration once John's form of literary expression is recognized.

titles, since they carried connotations of Jewish political and material aspirations that Jesus renounced. The reticence of Jesus to spell out his personal claims means that we face considerable difficulty in answering the question of his exclusiveness on the basis of his own direct claims for his person, i.e., who he was. We must look for more indirect evidence from his teaching and actions.

Certainly one of the amazing features of Jesus' teaching is the way in which he makes a person's ultimate destiny with God dependent upon that person's response to himself. "For whoever is ashamed of me and of my words in this adulterous and sinful generation, of him will the Son of man also be ashamed, when he comes in the glory of his Father" (Mark 8:38).[10] There is ultimate, that is, final significance in Jesus and his teaching because the ultimate consequences of life are linked to him. A correlation exists between the response to Jesus now and the response of God's eschatological agent to the individual in the culmination of history.

In other ways also, the teaching of Jesus discloses an implicit claim of uniqueness and finality. This is especially conspicuous in Jesus' manner of placing himself above the law by claiming to speak for the will of God so as to interpret the law rightly and even to set aside parts of it. (See especially the Sermon on the Mount.) Interpreters have noted that even the parables have an implicit Christological claim. In this light, the disputed statement of Jesus in Matthew 11:27 rings true: "All things have been delivered to me by my Father; and no one knows the Son except the Father, and no one knows the Father except the Son and any one to whom the Son chooses to reveal him."

These elements from Jesus' teaching point to a close linkage between the content of the message and the person of the messenger. Jesus has been given a message from

10. For purposes of our question, it makes no material difference where one stands on the meaning of "son of man" and whether Jesus identifies himself with the Son of Man or not. Compare and contrast Matthew 10:32,33 and Luke 12:8,9: "I" in Matthew is "Son of Man" in Luke, which is a similar but not parallel saying. The double attestation of the Marcan tradition and the special source (Q) of Matthew and Luke to this concept of one's status on the last day being dependent on present response to Jesus strengthens its claim to authenticity.

God of such final significance that one asks who this person is with such authority. On the other hand, statements like Matthew 11:27 just quoted speak expressly of the unique relationship of this person to God that grounds the teaching authority. On the occasion of his teaching about servanthood, Jesus used the example of the child but drops another astonishing statement of his mediatorial role for God himself: "Whoever receives one such child in my name receives me; and whoever receives me, receives not me but him who sent me" (Mark 9:37).

All of these features have their place within the larger theme of Jesus' message of the kingdom of God which has drawn near in his ministry. "The time is fulfilled, and the kingdom of God is at hand; repent, and believe in the gospel" (Mark 1:15). The presence of the kingdom is mediated in Jesus' teaching. It is also actualized in his ministry of healing and exorcism (Luke 11:20). Once again it is evident that the person and the ministry are inseparable. In the presence of this person, the kingdom of God is present. This appears to be the plain sense of Jesus' retort to the Pharisees in Luke 17:21 when they ask about the time of the kingdom's coming: ". . . the kingdom of God is in the midst of you." Jesus is the kingdom present.

With the concept of the kingdom there is an additional dimension. The time is fulfilled; the kingdom has drawn near. There is a note of finality here. This is not the finality of a message, or even of a person, although they are related. This is a finality of context: history has reached a point of completeness, a stage of maturity. The character of the time is different; it is unique. What is claimed in all this is not that some change in the external structures of history explains the special role of Jesus (in a manner rather like Jewish apocalyptic). Rather, it is the other way around. The historical presence of the person of Jesus modifies the character of the historical situation.[11] Where Jesus is, the situation changes for every person.

This is then the basis for the call to repentance that

11. This is not to deny the typical New Testament salvation history perspective that history, under the control of God, has moved to a point of being prepared for the ministry of Jesus (for example, Gal. 4:4 and Mark 1:15).

Jesus announces. Jesus asks all to repent. The implication of this must not escape us. Jesus does not see repentance as something just for the ungodly and the immoral. The righteous are eligible for repentance even though they tend to miss the point of Jesus' call. (Hence his statement that he came not to call the righteous but sinners to repentance.) A new offer of God is now present and all are called to reorient their lives (repent) to the new possibilities of righteousness in Jesus. It is not a question of what level of godliness one had reached or whether one had already experienced salvation. In Jesus, all, with no exception, are summoned to step into a new kingdom reality not possible before. (See the story in Luke 13:1-5.)

It would be preposterous to conclude that Jesus thought no salvation had preceded him in Israel (or the nations?) or that no saints existed during his lifetime before his ministry to them. However one understands the exclusiveness of Jesus, it is not a simple matter of salvation here, non-salvation elsewhere. One must speak of salvation in Jesus as final in the sense that it supersedes all previous modes of salvation. It fulfills the older in a manner analogous to Jesus' fulfillment of the law—the former is not negated, but is taken up into something greater. And, in this sense, it claims acceptance from all. This then is the basic paradigm with which we are to understand the exclusiveness of Jesus Christ.

A crucial question emerges at this point. Does this paradigm apply to all peoples and religions? What has just been described answers to the relation of Jesus to the older covenant with Israel. The idea of fulfillment itself is a salvation history concept and this concept is rooted in the special history of Israel's God saving this chosen people. We will return to this question at a later point. Here it will suffice to note that the early church understood the meaning of Jesus' life to be relevant for universal history, i.e., all nations.

In the light of the discussion above concerning repentance, the report in Acts 17 of Paul's sermon in Athens is particularly interesting and illuminating. At the conclusion of the sermon, Paul remarks, "The times of ignorance God overlooked, but now he commands all men everywhere to repent. . ." (Acts 17:30). Here is the call to repentance in the light of a changed situation brought about by God's action in Jesus. In this it parallels the preaching of Jesus himself. But now, the proclamation is directed to the Gentiles. According to the book of Acts then, the paradigm of final salvation in Jesus applies to all nations as well as Israel. But, with this example, we have passed over into the claims of the early church for Jesus' uniqueness.

The claims of the early church

What was a matter of reticence for Jesus, became a matter of bold statement and proclamation for the early church. In direct language and standard titles, the first believers speak of one whom God has exalted to his own right hand. The status of Jesus as Son of God is now plainly set forth in its rightful meaning and in effective demonstration by his resurrection from the dead (Rom. 1:4). The implied sonship of the Abba-relation of Jesus to God is now understood as sonship of the highest divine status (Phil. 2:9,10). The church not only is more explicit in its confession of Jesus the Christ; it now makes the person of Jesus Christ the starting point of the gospel, not the subtle presupposition of the message as in Jesus' own teaching. Therefore, we recognize that heightening of the Christological confession takes place and by consequence also a heightening of the exclusive claims for the person of Christ.[12]

12. We cannot probe into the currently burning question of whether the development of Christology in the early church and on into the patristic period in the great creeds is an authentic and authoritative one or not. That there is some kind of development is indisputable. In the present state of the question, this writer prefers the position of C.F.D. Moule in *The Origin of Christology* (New York: Cambridge University Press, 1977), who defends a consistent unfolding of understanding and articulation in the New Testament (development rather than evolution). Norman Kraus in his book, *Jesus Christ Our Lord* (Scottdale: Herald Press, 1987), has placed this whole matter on the Mennonite agenda. Kraus is right that an Anabaptist hermeneutic has no reason to defend the Christology of the patristic creeds *a priori*. We answer to the canonical writings; the creeds are open to criticism. In my opinion, we have no ultimate stake in the conceptual framework or language of these creeds. However, the experience of the church (tradition) is certainly of value to us. That experience indicates that the formulas of Chalcedon have withstood the testing of philosophical changes and attempts at theological restatement. Chalcedon has a resistant quality; it should be abandoned only on overwhelming evidence and after the clear construction of something better that communicates a "high Christology" able to elicit the adoration of Jesus Christ as living Lord. I have not found other approaches convincing in this respect. This is not to condemn the search, however.

In order to trace this confession of the uniqueness and finality of Jesus Christ, we will limit ourselves to two crucial contexts: the book of Acts and the prologue of John. Reference was made to the sermon of Paul at Athens, as recorded in Acts 17. We noted how the call to repentance has become a universal call to every person. In the sermon, this is anchored on one side in the resurrection (17:31) and on the other side in the monotheism of the Old Testament by which there is one creator God who unites all peoples in a common spiritual quest. The relevance of both of these presuppositions for the universal relevance of Jesus Christ can hardly be overemphasized. The resurrection is the sign beyond all signs that the highest of all salvation acts—the defeat of death—has been made a realistic expectation because of its accomplishment in human experience in history. A truly universal hope has been opened up. The early missionaries seem to reflect the conviction that such a message would find no rival claim and should be withheld from no one. On the other hand, the belief in the one God leads to a view of oneness in human experience. All peoples come from the one source and have a common destiny in this God. In this way, the early church builds a bridge of solidarity with all persons and nations by means of which they share the novelty of God's final saving acts in Jesus of Nazareth.

However, this sharing is not done in Paul's sermon (or elsewhere in Acts) by an absolute polarity of negative and positive, in which the other religion is completely negated. The religiosity of the Athenians is an expression of the search for the one God. Moreover, is there not even a sign of grace in the comment, as fascinating as it is enigmatic, that God has overlooked the former times of ignorance, but now commands repentance? Behind the description of ignorance, which does not have the connotation of stupidity but of unawareness, is a God who shows patience and mercy towards those without knowledge.[13] Parallel ideas to these are found in Acts 14:16-17: "In past generations he (God) allowed all the nations to walk in their own ways; yet he did not leave himself without witness, for he did

13. Compare the ideas of Paul in the second chapter of Romans.

good. . . ." The theme of God's patient indulgence is repeated here. The assertion of God's positive blessing is stated
more strongly by reference to acts of goodness leading to a
fulfilled life. This is quite a generous view of God's dealing
with those outside both the Christian and the Jewish
streams of salvation.

It is not the practice of the Bible to use the language of
salvation for this general blessing of God to the nations.
Presumably that language is intended to carry the special
meaning of the deliverance acts accomplished on behalf of
the elect people. When today the question is posed whether
salvation is found outside of Christ, the term *salvation* is
being used more widely. The Acts passages give us ground
for saying that God does accept and bless (and, in this
sense, saves) in other traditions. For many, including conservative Christians, the term *salvation* refers to the final
destiny of the individual. While this is a partial understanding from the biblical point of view, the question is
important. What is striking in this regard is that biblical
writers do not press this question, one way or the other. It
is as if they respect the freedom and sovereignty of God
and refrain from judgment. This observation needs to be
qualified carefully. The biblical writers believe in the separation of the righteous and wicked in eternity; but they
show no inclination to make these lines of separation synonymous with the lines of the covenant people. The wicked
will perish; but never is there the simple equation of the
nations with the wicked.[14]

14. It is appropriate to raise the question whether the biblical expressions that
speak of the lack of righteousness in every individual do not mean that apart from
the right making (justification) in Jesus all will perish. This implication drawn from
the concept of justification is strong among churches of the Reformation tradition.
Jesus' statement that "unless you repent you will all likewise perish" (Luke 13:5)
seems to say the same thing. This is not easy to reconcile with the kind of viewpoint
we are seeing in Acts. A possible resolution lies in the perspective on repentance
described above in the setting of Jesus' life. When the announcement of final salvation in Jesus comes, then a new decision for or against God must be made. To reject
the kingdom offered by Jesus the Christ is to turn definitively from God. This warn-
ing would not need to imply that all who have not encountered the Jesus claim are
destined to perish. In any event, even when we take seriously the biblical, and especially Pauline, analysis of the sinfulness of every human person, we still must reck-
on with the religious sentiment found not only in biblical religion that a person is
not perfect or worthy before God and therefore calls upon the mercy of God.

There is evidence in Acts, as in the life of Jesus, that
no need is felt to limit God's saving interest and interven-
tion in other peoples. What is felt is a compelling drive to
share the *final* salvation of Jesus that supersedes all other
knowledge and experience with God. In Acts, the God-
fearing Cornelius is just such an example (Acts 10:1, 2).
He is a devout man who fears God. Peter makes the
astounding comment at the moment of his meeting Cornelius: "Truly I perceive that God shows no partiality, but
in every nation any one who fears him and does what is
right is acceptable to him" (10:34, 35). With the language
of acceptance used here, one could hardly affirm that Cornelius was a subject of God's eternal rejection outside of
Christ. But just as important is the fact that God does not
hold back from Cornelius a greater salvation. The forgiveness of sin in Jesus and the blessing of the Spirit—both
signs of God's final salvation—are appropriate to Cornelius
without negating the acceptance of any earlier time.

But what about that classical passage on our subject in
Acts 4:12 to the effect that there is salvation in no other for
there is no other name known to the human race by which
we must be saved? Does that not have the obvious meaning that no one can be saved unless they know the name of
Jesus? How does this relate to Acts 10, 14, and 17? Some
light is thrown on the matter when we consider the meaning of the word *must* in Luke/Acts. This is a common word
to the author, having a special theological meaning. It
points to the purposes of God which are being realized in
the movement of events in Israel, Jesus, the church, and
the world. The *must* in our verse does not refer to an
intrinsic logic of reality as if there is no material possibility
of salvation elsewhere. Rather, it is God's intention that,
at this stage in the fulfillment of his purposes, all persons
might be summoned to faith in Jesus. This kind of salvation exists in no other. Such an understanding of the verse
would then parallel the proclamation of Jesus regarding
the kingdom whose approach has called for reorientation
on the part of all, even the righteous.

A further, fascinating implication of this understanding
is that the *must* of this salvation bears not only upon the
hearer of the gospel but lays upon the believer a sense of

obligation to proclaim this message which God intends for all nations. We believers are involved in the process of fulfilling the grand design of the Lord of history. A divine necessity has been laid upon us.

Beyond any doubt, the book of Acts represents the concerns of a Christian mind that wrestled with the relationship of the particularity of the means of salvation in Jesus of Nazareth and the universality of the mission of the church to all peoples. The stories show clearly a church that is responding to how the exclusive claim of the message (no other name) relates to the universal religious experience of humankind (anyone who fears God is acceptable).

Another key passage of the New Testament which reveals the same interest is the prologue to the Gospel of John. In all probability, the evangelist has chosen the concept of *logos* (word) to bridge between the wisdom tradition of the Old Testament (salvation history) and the philosophical tradition of the Greco-Roman world (universal history). Jesus is that bridge: the Word which became flesh in the particular man Jesus is also the creative agent of God from which comes all life and light in every age. This Word "enlightens every man" (John 1:9). These qualities of life and light are the very qualities that Jesus brings in the gospel. Our author is prepared to see these gospel values linked to some degree with the universal experience of humankind. Here we see a new kind of theological development in which the exclusiveness of Jesus Christ, which disclosed itself out of the life and message of one person in a particular historical setting, is projected backward in time and outward in space. Now the true and the right of Israel's saving history *and* of the entire human race—the total creation—are shown to be grounded in Jesus Christ. A new bold step is taken; not only is final salvation found in Jesus Christ, but all penultimate salvation is from him as well.

Nevertheless, the prologue does not leave us with a positive picture of the condition of that universal world. Light is in conflict with darkness. When the light came into the world, it was more likely rejected than received. The general picture of humanity outside of Christ, no matter what evidence of light and life there may be, is one of

16

disobedience and failure. This outlook is shared by other scriptural writers. Especially Paul, in his letter to the Romans, articulates this viewpoint. God has made himself plain to all so that all are without excuse. The Gentiles may have a law on their hearts that may "perhaps excuse them on that day" of judgment (Rom. 2:15). Still "all men, both Jews and Greeks, are under the power of sin" (Rom. 3:9) and therefore proper objects of the liberating grace of God in Jesus. In fact, it is the death of Jesus that reveals the degree of spiritual death of every person. "We are convinced that one has died for all; therefore all have died" (2 Cor. 5:14).

In summary, the range of New Testament teaching we have examined indicates that the early Christian outlook did not negate the presence of good in other cultural and religious settings. How God will judge these persons is not a matter of specific speculation. There is the recognition that moral uprightness is found among all nations and that God finds this a ground for his favor even in the final judgment. "God shows no partiality" is the ruling principle (Acts 10:34 and Rom. 2:11, both in the same contexts cited above). On the other hand, a new work of salvation has occurred in Jesus of Nazareth, the Messiah of God, that surpasses all other ways of knowing God. To withhold this news from anyone is unconscionable. To announce this saving message is *both* to render the hearer more responsible before God *and* to offer him/her a new dimension of hope not known or experienced before. Here both sinner and saint, according to other religious and moral standards, are summoned to a radical turning in adjusting their lives to a new Master. This is the exclusiveness of Jesus Christ.

The implications for the church's practice of mission

The question to which we now turn is how we as believers in our time and place shall respond to the claims of this Lord. There are two areas which will be explored. The treatment will be only introductory in nature.

17

That there is a degree of scandal in the exclusive claim of Jesus Christ is undeniable for the person of modern sensitivities and for many persons of deep moral sensitivity in any age. If this claim were the projection on Jesus of our self-worship and cultural imperialism it would be most despicable. As it is, the claim comes from One who impresses all who encounter him as humble of spirit and sterling in moral integrity. Jesus Christ himself places before us the either-or of decision without obvious evidence on which to reject him and without unambiguous proof by which to guarantee him. We can only accept (or reject) him and live within the ensuing demonstration of the good of his claims. As a finite human, I cannot master the absolute claim of exclusiveness. It is unattainable and unverifiable for me. I can only receive and experience it for what it is in itself. The problem of the exclusiveness of Jesus Christ is after all a question of faith.

We do find, however, some perspective on the whole matter from two areas to which we ought to give more careful attention than before.

Universal and particular. We must sharpen our understanding of the relationship between a theology of creation and a theology of redemption. Woven throughout the presentation of the biblical evidence there have been allusions to this issue. The biblical story of salvation is one of specific acts of God in history for a particular people in a concrete time and place. Salvation is particular. This perspective is the dominant one of the biblical narrative—but not the only one. There is also the story of God's concern and responsibility for all of creation. There is a universal history of salvation. One can trace the unfolding of this double perspective in the Old Testament as the conviction of absolute monotheism emerges in Israel paralleled by a heightened emphasis on God as maker of heaven and earth. The shared wisdom of all people is incorporated into Israel's faith. In the New Testament, the movement is from the Messianic salvation of Jesus for Israel to the universal mission. We have seen the evidence of the theological development in response to this movement in Acts and John. Thus the particular and the universal co-exist in biblical revelation.

There is a kind of "ugly ditch"[15] that easily opens up between these perspectives. Taken alone, the particularistic stream (cf. special revelation) becomes sectarian and exclusivistic, unable to see truth and good elsewhere and uninterested in the sharing of its truth, to say nothing of learning from others. On the other side, the universalistic stream (cf. general revelation) alone tends towards syncretism, bland inclusivism and indifferent tolerance, unable to accept a view of God who allows truth to be conditioned by the historical process. By holding on to the value of both perspectives, the Bible gives us a clue about how to think and act rightly, even though the implications are often not worked out. Put in the broadest of terms, the mission of Christ's community takes the stance of anticipating and acknowledging the activity of the creator God in every place while at the same time openly telling its own story.[16] God, and the working of God's Spirit, will have always preceded his people in their mission; the latter mission must harmonize with the former.

Finite and infinite. We must learn to live creatively with the tension between the finality of Christ and the finitude of the church—and never ease the tension. Practically speaking, the deepest scandal in our commitment to exclusiveness is not the claim of exclusiveness of Jesus Christ but the burden for the followers of Christ to represent his exclusiveness through the actions and structures of finite history and imperfect humanity.

It is true that the idea of incarnation, in which the infinite and the finite unite, involves the same dilemma. For the non-Christian, this too is a scandal. For the person outside of faith, there is a tendency to lump these two levels of the question together—all of the Christian religion

15. The reference, of course, is to Lessing's phrase which contrasts the universal truths of reason and the particular truths of history. This is the philosophical problem that parallels our present discussion and is a backdrop to it. See, for example, the discussion in Edward Schillebeeckx, *Jesus: An Experiment in Christology*, Vintage Books (New York: Random House, 1981), p. 583f.

16. This viewpoint is well expressed in the title and content of Lesslie Newbigin's book *The Open Secret* (Grand Rapids: Eerdmans, 1978).

appears to claim exclusiveness and is judged accordingly. For the believer, *at the theoretical level*, a clear distinction is made between the finality of Christ and the human condition of the church in all of its aspects. *At the experiential level*, however, it is quite another matter. As for the nonbeliever so for the believer, the two dimensions easily are confused. The result of this blurred distinction is one or the other of two opposite distortions of our missionary stance. In both instances the quality of finality is attributed (erroneously) to the church as a religious phenomenon. The one distortion is a pretentious attitude of superiority that is readily accompanied by the abusive use of power to achieve one's ends since one is playing the part of God for the world. The other distortion is a falsely assumed inferiority that is ashamed of being associated with anything claiming exclusiveness.

Both of these distortions are alive and well in the church. I sense that for the Anabaptist tradition churches it is the second one that is more insidious today. What happens is that we identify ourselves too closely with the claim of Christ as if we are responsible for it. When traditional Anabaptist humility mixes with modern relativism (of the kind described above), a powerful impulse is created to distance ourselves from any appearance of exclusiveness. But no authority has been granted us to create such a claim, and no authorization has been granted us to dismantle it. This claim belongs to Jesus of Nazareth who is now exalted Lord. He must answer for himself—or rather, every person must answer to this claim for himself/herself.

Still, this is not a simple matter. In a fundamental sense, the exclusiveness of Jesus Christ is not transmitted to his followers. It is a nontransferable trait. Yet we cannot disassociate ourselves from it. The church as a new community is to demonstrate the more-than-they level of righteousness (Matt. 5) that is made possible because of the empowerment of Christ's final salvation. Also, we are to be messengers of this claim and the listener will be hard put to appreciate a distinction between message and messenger. In a derivative sense, therefore, the church participates in Christ's finality. However, we can at best be merely a sign, not a sample of that finality. This role will never become easy. It is a burden; but woe to us if the burden is not carried.

Faithful practice

What will the practice of mission look like when it reflects the preceding perspective on the claims of its Lord? We will offer only three basic theses.

The self-understanding is apostolic. The characteristic self-consciousness of the biblical messenger is that of the reluctant draftee. This trait ought not be passed off as a sign of weak faith. More profoundly, it is an awareness of the contradiction between a divine claim of such greatness and a human instrument of such weakness. Any other attitude would prove that the individual is out of touch. The sense of being sent, i.e., the apostolic consciousness, is the only legitimate condition under which a mission in the name of a unique Savior can be carried forward. That the self-awareness of an authentic witness is not grounded in any sense of pretentiousness is illustrated by the curious tendency to see oneself as a debtor (Rom. 1:14). The messenger is not a profiteer and the style is not exploitative when all sense of creditorship is absent. The exclusiveness of Jesus Christ is not a problem at the level of self-consciousness of the one who is motivated by a mandate outside oneself. Embarrassment at such a claim can only be a sign that our sense of call is more humanly derived than divinely impressed upon us.

Our stance is mediatorial. The typical biblical metaphors for those in the mission of God are *messenger* and *witness.* In both instances, the roles so described are ones in which the authorization rests outside of the communicator. The messenger is sent by a person in authority, the witness is empowered by having seen or experienced an external event or person. The truth of these persons is mediated. To communicate a claim of finality from within oneself is absurd for a finite human being. Absoluteness is something which I as a human being can neither ground nor demonstrate, I can only pass on such a claim as a witness or messenger from an absolute source.

There is a certain freedom then over against the question of Christ's exclusiveness. Although we have staked our lives on this truth, we are not responsible to answer for it, nor to determine the future shape of historical events in order to fulfill the claim. How God, in history or beyond it, will make good on the finality of his Son and how this will affirm or deny other religious systems is mine to observe more than to determine. "We cannot but speak of what we have seen and heard" (Acts 4:20)—if indeed we have been so moved by the hand of God.

Our style is irenic. It is surprising that we in the peace church tradition have not made more of our peace theme as a criterion for our evangelism and mission. Peace tends to be viewed as one part of the mission, less as a way of doing all mission. In the English language, we have the word *irenic* which comes from the Greek word for peace. When, therefore, we speak of an irenic style, we are not calling on general usage for its meaning. We mean to pour into the word all the biblical content of peace which implies both a goal and a way of attaining the goal. In mission, "the harvest of righteousness is sown in peace by those who make peace" (James 3:18).

Irenic witness to the claims of Christ is one that takes its strong, unapologetic stand on the stage of history to be seen and heard. It is strong in commitment and conviction without resorting to psychological manipulation or external coercion. Just, as in instances of suffering evil, we defer to the retribution of God, so in our mission, once we have shared the story of God's grace to us in Jesus, we defer to the visitation of God's spirit in the listener to persuade. An irenic witness can afford to exercise great patience while the Lord works. This witness can also be dialogic in style, because it realizes its human need to listen and learn with respect for fellow human seekers, being confident that the monologic address of the divine call comes authentically from God alone. The irenic witness is wise as a serpent and as harmless as a dove (Matt. 10:16).

Exclusive truth in Jesus the Christ

Out of a review of the biblical sources, we have attempted a defense of the exclusiveness of Jesus Christ. Put tersely, the biblical claim is this: *God's conclusive* revelation and action in Jesus the Christ gives to this One an *exclusive* dimension of truth which, because of its universal relevance, is *inclusive* of all humanity.

The fact that this saving action in Jesus takes place in the midst of a history in which God is universally at work means that truth is not the sole possession of the tradition of this Jesus. It does, however, signify that a truth is here revealed that bears a finality beside which all other claims are made second best.

The followers of this way are called to share this truth, this way of salvation, with all others without passing judgment on the value of their faiths or the question of their eternal destiny (apart from self-evident wickedness). The irony of a finite people bearing a final message must not be forgotten or dissolved away by absolutizing the church or relativizing the claim. The scandal of Christ's exclusiveness is to be embraced with faithfulness, humbly but joyfully.

Competing Christologies
Response to "The Exclusiveness of Jesus Christ"

Daniel D. García Swartzentruber

First, I will briefly analyze seven Christological formulations which tend to call into question the exclusiveness of Christ. The first five are expressions of what Brother Brunk calls fundamentalism. The last two are manifestations of what he has described as the relativism of our times. This will show the context in which we are called to proclaim the exclusiveness of Christ. Since I come from Argentina, and since the background of his paper has to do with the problem of proclaiming the the Christologies I know from Latin America. But you will easily find a connection with the North American situation.

In the second part, I shall make some comments on Brother Brunk's analysis of New Testament materials and on his missiological suggestions.

I am not a theologian. I am merely a historian. So my response will be more historic than theological.

The Christology of the Hispanic conquest and colonization

The "discovery" of America by Spain was interpreted from the beginning in religious terms. Jose Miguez Bonino, a well-known Argentine theologian, said that "in Spain there existed something akin to a temporal messianism" in which the destiny of the nation and the destiny of the church were believed to be united. Hispanic Christianity, it was believed, was unique in that the nation had been selected by God to be the instrument for the *salvation* of the world.

In this context, the exclusiveness of Christ was replaced by the exclusiveness of Hispanic culture as unsurpassable, unique, definitive mediation between God and humankind. The salvific meaning of Hispanism was asserted as over against the Indian culture and religion, which was considered as absolutely empty of value and virtue. What was involved here was a *tabula rasa* policy that totally dislodged the Indian culture. When you absolutize a historical mediation, it is easy to fall prey to the temptation of violence. You feel the need to promote at any cost the victory of your exclusive historical project, which is the unparalleled means of salvation.

The images of Christ produced by Indian and mestizo art in the seventeenth and eighteenth centuries give account of the process I have described. There was the suffering Christ symbolizing the defeated Indian culture; there was also the exalted Christ, the image of the divinized Spanish conqueror. The exclusiveness of Christ as unsurpassable means of salvation had been replaced by the exclusiveness of Hispanic culture and those were the consequences.

The Christology of Roman Catholicism

In this case, the exclusiveness of Christ has been displaced by the exclusiveness of the institutional church. "Outside the church there is no salvation." The church, interpreted in hierarchical categories, is seen as the bearer of the meaning of history. The church, i.e., the hierarchy, dispenses objective grace to everybody who comes asking for it. Again, Christ does not count as unsurpassable means of salvation; final salvation is monopolized by another historical mediation, in this case a religious one.

The images of Christ emerging from this situation tend to identify Christ with the hierarchical apparatus. The priest is the *alter Christus*. And the pope is the ultimate representative of Christ on earth.

The exclusiveness of the institutional church manifests itself in the miracle of transubstantiation. If you want to receive Christ, you can do it during the mass. The bread *is* his body, and the wine *is* his blood. But again: who is the mediator between you and salvation (i.e., objective grace)? The hierarchy, in which the power to effect transubstantiation resides. Christ as unparalleled means of salvation has been replaced again by a historical mediation.

The Christology of Protestant evangelization

Now I am talking about the Protestant North American missionaries who came to Latin America at the beginning of this century. The modernizing, liberal elites that took power at the end of the nineteenth century regarded Catholicism as a basic obstacle in the path of progress toward modernity. They regarded Protestantism as an ally in their own cause because they perceived it as the religion of freedom, individualism, private judgment, education, and personal morality.

It seems to me that Protestantism claimed and assumed the role that the Latin American liberal elites had assigned it in the transition to a new society. In doing so, many of these missionaries tended to replace the exclusiveness of Jesus Christ by the exclusiveness of a new historical mediation: the North American culture. They filled up their own culture with salvific content. Roman Catholicism was seen as cause, bearer, and consequence of the feudal period, those Dark Ages characterized by social and political oppression, obscurantism, ignorance, and cultural lag. That was hell. The North American culture, including democracy, education, scientific and technical progress, freedom, and individual rights was heaven. Catholicism was *religion*; Protestantism was *faith*, according to W. Stanley Rycroft.

The images of Christ that developed out of this context were the Christ of individualism, the Christ of subjectivity, the Christ of Calvinist moral virtues: industry, honesty, moderation, frugality. Once more the exclusiveness of Jesus Christ as unsurpassable means of salvation had given way to the exclusiveness of a historical, cultural mediation.

The Christology of sectarianism

In this case I am referring to the theology and practice of

26

many religious transnational corporations dedicated to the evangelization of the world. What you find here is that the exclusiveness of Christ is replaced by the exclusiveness of a preacher or of a method. Final salvation is not in Christ but in the preacher who is able to mediate Christ to you. Final salvation does not reside in Christ but in the method you have to follow in order to enter heaven. Christ as unparalleled means of salvation has been dislodged. Here it is a matter of the miraculous power of the preacher-showman, or the mysterious salvific power of a set of rules.

The images of Christ emerging out of this theology and practice of mission is what Bonhoeffer called "the Christ of boundary situations." People are psychologically forced to see themselves as the worst persons in the world, they are invited to hate themselves for what they are, they are prompted to think seriously of the possibility of a sudden death (which would be the door to eternal damnation). In synthesis, people are forced to see themselves in a boundary situation. The preachers' presupposition is that in this situation people will turn to Jesus Christ as their last resort and be converted. Bonhoeffer called this a religious violation.

Again, the exclusiveness of Christ is displaced, or is made dependent upon the peculiar situation in which the hearers are forced to see themselves, i.e., a boundary or crisis situation.

The Christology of liberation

The danger of calling in question the exclusiveness of Christ as unsurpassable means of salvation is also present, in my opinion, in the well-known liberation theology. The historical mediation which Roman Catholic liberation theologians tend to absolutize is the project of democratic socialism. The features of this project are, according to Gustavo Gutierrez, the following: social appropriation of the means of production, social appropriation of political powEr social appropriation of freedom, and creation of a new social consciousness. J. L. Segundo in *Capitalism vs Socialism: Crux Theologica* criticizes European political theologians such as J. Moltmann and J. Metz for, in his view, failing to understand the kind of relationship that exists between historical mediations and the kingdom of God. Segundo asserts that democratic socialism is neither an analogy nor a metaphor of the kingdom: it is the *cause* of the kingdom, the historical project which opens the way for the advent of this kingdom. "Outside democratic socialism there is no salvation." Some of these theologians certainly run the risk of falling into a new version of Roman Catholic political sacramentarianism.

The Christ of some liberation theologians is the Christ of social transformation, the Christ of revolution, the Christ of democratic socialism. Once more the exclusiveness of Christ has been replaced by the emphasis laid upon the salvific virtues of a historical mediation.

The Christology of democratic capitalism

Here we come to what Brother Brunk calls the relativism of our age. Peter Berger has spoken of this phenomenon in terms of the death of ideologies. Friedrich Hayek in *Law, Legislation, and Liberty* has described the free society as a "pluralistic society without a common hierarchy of ends." He says, "It is often made the reproach to the Great Society and its market order that it lacks an agreed ranking of ends. This, however, is in fact its great merit which makes individual freedom and all its values possible. . . . The decisive step which made such peaceful collaboration possible is the absence of concrete common purposes and the adoption of barter of exchange." If I don't misunderstand him, he is saying that the basis of modern relativism is the market order.

And we do have a Christology of the market order. Michael Novak in *The Spirit of Democratic Capitalism* says, "One of the most *poignant* lessons of the Incarnation is the difficult teaching that one must learn to be humble, think concretely, face facts, train oneself to realism. . . . The Incarnation is a doctrine of hope but not of utopia. The point of Incarnation is to respect the world as it is, to acknowledge its limits. . .and to disbelieve any promises that the world is now/or ever will be transformed into the City of God. The world is not going to become—ever—a kingdom of justice and love."

In this case, the exclusiveness of Christ is replaced by the exclusiveness of the market order; the final salvation is to be found only in democratic capitalism. The Christology of the market order is a Christology of realism: this Christ is conservative, anti-utopian. In my opinion, in Novak, the individualism and the consequent relativism of our age become sacred: relativism transforms itself into a new expression of fundamentalism. "Outside democratic capitalism there is no salvation."

The Christology of the peculiar-but-not-final Christ

Since the Second World Missionary Conference (Jerusalem, 1928) there has been a theological development which has also called in question the exclusiveness of Christ as unsurpassable means of salvation. In Jerusalem, there was deep preoccupation with regard to the progress of secularism. In this context, many asserted that Christian missions should abandon their aggressive profile as over-against non- Christian religions, in order to give way to a peaceful cooperation against the common enemy: secularism. This position was afterwards radicalized. In 1932, the philosopher of religion Ernest Hocking in *Re-Thinking Missions: A Laymen's Inquiry After One Hundred Years* pleaded for a new understanding of mission. Christians should see themselves as members of a world religious system in which every religion made its contribution in order to set up a peaceful and just society. The proclamation of the exclusiveness of Christ had to be given up if this cooperation between religions was to become a reality. The goal of world historical evolution, Hocking went on, was the fusion of all religions into one universal, human religion possessing the final truth and salvation. This proposal was complemented afterward by the phenomenology of religion approach. According to it, we can easily identify analogous concepts, beliefs, and rites in the different world religions. Therefore, it is concluded, the basic unity of all religions must be asserted.

In this context, it is not possible to affirm the exclusiveness of Christ. He might be peculiar, in the same way as the prophets, leaders, and founders of many other religions are. But he cannot claim exclusiveness as unparalleled means of salvation.

The exclusiveness of Christ: the New Testament evidence

It is in the context of all these Christologies which tend to call into question the exclusiveness of Christ, that we must evaluate the useful contribution George Brunk III has made to our theological reflection and missionary practice. I would like to add some comments to his incisive analysis of the New Testament materials.

1. An important aspect of New Testament theology is that the proclamation of the exclusiveness of Christ calls into question the claims of every historical and cultural mediation, even that of Judaism. Since Jesus has come, salvation has to do with God's grace manifested through his Messiah, and not the fact of belonging to a particular tradition and culture.

2. However, Brunk rightly asserts that New Testament Christians appeal to cultural and religious mediations in order to share the gospel. Paul considered that "the religiosity of the Athenians was an expression of the search for the one God." Besides, who could deny the significance Judaism has for the New Testament writers as cultural mediation that prepared the way for the Messiah? My point here is that New Testament Christians did not implement a *tabula rasa* policy. They rejected the absolute and final claims of historical mediations, but appealed to them in order to reach men and women with the message of the exclusiveness of Christ.

3. Brunk rightly observed that in the biblical writings there is no systematic defense of the exclusiveness of Christ as a theoretical problem over against other religions. As John Driver has shown us with regard to the atonement, the attempt to systematize does not appear in Scripture: it is rooted in western patterns of thought and it has strongly influenced the development of western theology. Anyway, I would like to point out that some of the most valuable contributions to a systematic interpretation of non-Christian religions in biblical perspective come from a theological tradition linked to the names of Paul Althaus,

Emil Brunner, Hendrik Kraemer, Gerhard Rosenkranz, Walter Freytag, and, more recently, Peter Beyerhaus. These theologians, opposing both the relativization of Christianity in the religio-historical school and the Barthian denial of the theological relevance of comparative religious studies, have advocated a dialectical understanding of non-Christian religions. These religions are seen as expressions *both* of humanity's unquenchable thirst for God *and* humanity's sinful rebellion. This view has been complemented by Karl Heim, who has added a third forgotten factor towards a biblical understanding of non-Christian religions: the manifestation of demonic forces in them. This theological tradition could help us to go beyond the Christology of the peculiar-but-not-final Christ.

4. Brunk rightly notes that the claims of the early church with regard to the exclusiveness of Christ were not supported in any way by the exertion of psychological or physical coercion. He is making an important point here: since it was the exclusiveness of *that* particular Messiah, Jesus of Nazareth, the one that was being claimed, the way of claiming it was to be in accordance with the historical shape of Christ's mission. The hearer could not be forced to accept the exclusiveness of that Messiah.

The exclusiveness of Christ: missiological suggestions

Finally, I would like to add some comments to Brunk's missiological suggestions.

1. Brunk correctly asserts that although we have staked our lives on the exclusiveness of Christ, we are not responsible to answer for it, nor to determine the shape of historical events in order to fulfill the claim. I think this observation can free us from falling prey to the temptation to resort to theocratic violence in order to vindicate God's cause in the world.

2. Brunk rightly observes that we should make more of our peace theme as a criterion for our evangelism and mission. There are two questions involved here. How can we be pluralistic without being relativistic? How can we proclaim the exclusiveness of Christ without being psychologically or morally violent?

Many sixteenth century Anabaptists could be pluralistic without falling into relativism and they could proclaim the exclusiveness of Christ without resorting to coercion because they had learned that the content and form of mission are one and the same, and both are determined by the example of Jesus.

3. Brunk suggests that we must learn to live creatively with the tension between the finality of Christ and the finitude of the church. As Anabaptists, we run the risk of falling into a new fundamentalism: we are tempted to identify the exclusiveness of Christ with the exclusiveness of the community of believers. We can overcome this temptation if we keep in mind that we are far from being a perfect mediation, that there is and there will always be an eschatological distance between the kingdom and the church. The church is not and will never be the kingdom!

4. Finally, the question I would like to pose is a paraphrase of Bonhoeffer's question: how can we speak of the exclusiveness of Christ in a secular world, in an autonomous world, in a world which has come of age? Bonhoeffer says there is "a decisive difference between Christianity and all religion. Man's religiosity makes him look in his distress to the power of God in the world. . . . The Bible, however, directs him to the powerlessness and suffering of God; only a suffering God can help." And then he says, "It is not some religious act which makes a Christian what he is, but participation in the suffering of God in the life of the world."

This world come of age may not be ready to listen to us when we proclaim the exclusiveness of Christ. The best way of sharing this message, without words, might be to participate in the suffering of God in the life of the world: "Für andere da sein." Bonhoeffer said, "To be there for others" as Jesus was.

Jesus Christ, the convener of the church

John E. Toews

Christology is the Mennonite agenda of the 1980s. This is
the third inter-Mennonite study conference on the topic.
The first, a believers' church conference, was held at
Bluffton College in 1980[1]; the second at the Associated
Mennonite Biblical Seminaries in 1988.[2] The first two were
preoccupied with the relationship of the classical creeds to
Anabaptist understandings of Christology. The dominant
agenda was the nature of Christ. Are the classical formulations of Christology helpful and appropriate for Mennonite
ecclesiological and ethical concerns?

Between the two conferences, the first two books on
Christology by Mennonites were published: John Driver,
*Understanding the Atonement for the Mission of the
Church* (1986), and C. Norman Kraus, *Jesus Christ Our
Lord* (1987). Driver focuses on the meaning of Christ's
death, while Kraus attempts a more thoroughgoing Christological formulation. Both come out of the missiological
scene and both seek to interpret New Testament Christology in fresh categories.

This is the first conference of the decade that seems not
to be shaped by the classical agenda. Although the paper
writers received no rationale for the topics, the agenda

---

1. See "A Believers' Church Christology," by J. Denny Weaver in *Mennonite
Quarterly Review* (1983), pp. 112-31.
2. See *Occasional Papers* 13, Institute of Mennonite Studies, 1989.

seems to be shaped by the missiological concerns of the church in the modern world. The key theological issue in missions and interfaith dialogue is the uniqueness of Christ. Is Christ the only way to salvation? Do other faiths represent valid ways to salvation?

While Anabaptists and Mennonites believed that Christ is normative for Christian ethics and church life, that understanding was not shared in ecumenical circles. Thanks to John H. Yoder's forceful argument for the normativeness of Jesus in ethics, the question has become a major point of discussion in modern Christian ethics and missions.

And, finally, does Christ have anything to do with the church? Mainstream Protestantism and evangelicalism both teach that Jesus preached the kingdom and we got the church. The church is an afterthought; it is not integral to Jesus' proclamation of the kingdom. Christology and ecclesiology are not explicitly linked. Biblical scholars continue to write volumes on Christology that say nothing about the church.[3] Mennonites assume there is an intimate relationship, but we have not addressed it confessionally or Christologically. This topic at this conference suggests we think it is time to make explicit an implicit theological understanding.

The issue for this paper has been defined as Christ the convener of the church. The language "convener of the church" is strange but fresh. While the terminology was not defined, it is assumed that the issue to be addressed is the relationship of Christology and ecclesiology. What does Christ have to do with the church? Does our understanding of the nature and mission of Christ shape our view of the church?

The starting point

We start with the New Testament, not the creeds. The reason is simple. Not only is the New Testament the starting point for Mennonite theological reflection, but the creeds are not explicitly helpful for our topic.

3. Arland J. Hultgren, *Christ and His Benefits*; Marinus de Jonge, *Christology in Context*; Earl Richard, *Jesus: One and Many*.

The creeds or confessions, ecumenical and Mennonite, assumed a relationship between Christology and ecclesiology. The relationship is implicit, not explicit. The churches wrote creeds or confessions of faith to summarize the essentials of the faith, as they understood it, given the issues of their time. The churches made Christological confessions because they viewed such claims as foundational for the life of the church. Furthermore, the churches making creeds or confessions in the past, whether churches of Christendom or sectarianism, had some sense of theological centeredness and communal cohesiveness.

We ask about the relationship between Christology and ecclesiology today because we live in a confessional situation: the assumptions of the Christian faith and the church are under challenge. The church today is uncertain about what is foundational, and the church has lost its sense of theological center and communal cohesiveness. The role and authority of creeds and confessions are questioned. What once was implicit must be made explicit for the life and direction of the church in such times.

The creeds or confessions are not helpful for a second reason: the Christology of the creeds represents the thought and language of a particular time in history. Their theological affirmations served the churches of their era. But the language is neither biblical nor modern, let alone post-modern. Furthermore, as scholars have pointed out, the creeds do not offer good Christologies, nor were they intended to. The ecumenical creeds were never designed as Christologies. Instead, they answered specific and narrow Christological questions of their time, e.g., was Jesus both human and divine? They outline rules for doing Christology but not Christology itself. They inform us that to deny certain things about Jesus is to be non-Christian in the presuppositions of our Christological thinking.[4]

Precisely because the classical creeds are not Christologies, we have noted the lack of explicit linkage between their limited Christological affirmations and ecclesiology.

4. George A. Lindbeck, *The Nature of Doctrine*; Marlin Miller, "Christological Concepts of the Classical Creeds and Mennonite Confessions of Faith"; Ben Ollenburger, "Christology and Creeds."

The creeds do not confess "Christ as the convener of the church" because they are concerned with the being of Christ (ontology), not the role or function of Christ. They either assume that Christ is the founder of the church or they address different questions, or both.

What is true of the ecumenical creeds is also true of the Mennonite confessions of faith. None of the major Mennonite confessions affirm "Christ as the convener of the church."[5] The Mennonite churches implicitly believe that Christ is "the convener of the church," and they preach that he is. But this conviction has not been articulated in the confessions because it was never a question.

We are asking a new question because we live in uncertain times. The new question requires that what was once implicit, maybe even in different ways in different confessional traditions, must now become explicit. New questions call us to return to the authoritative writings to inquire about direction.

But we must confess immediately that to start with the New Testament does not resolve all the issues. The New Testament is a diverse body of writings. We still have to decide where we start within the New Testament. Modern biblical Christological study has been preoccupied with two themes: 1) the Christological titles (e.g., Christ, Lord, Son of God) on the assumption that the titles disclose the nature of Christ; and 2) the origins and development of Christology from the earliest to the latest on the assumption that historical study will permit us to differentiate the primitive and pure from subsequent accretions. Recently, scholars have developed interest in the Christology of the various New Testament writers.[6] Most modern Christology distinguishes the person and the work of Christ.[7] The person Christologies examine the titles, creeds, and being statements to understand who Christ was, while studies on the work of Christ explain the meaning of Christ's

5. Howard Loewen, *One Lord, One Church, One Hope, and One God: Mennonite Confessions of Faith.*
6. De Jonge, *Christology in Context*; Hultgren, *Christ and His Benefits*; and Richard, *Jesus: One and Many.*
7. Hultgren, *Christ and His Benefits.*

death. None of these approaches focus the linkage between Christ and the church, between Christology and ecclesiology.

If we want to make the case for Christ as the convener of the church we will have to start at a different point. The proposal of this paper is that we start with Jesus himself. How did Jesus define his mission, as recorded in the Gospels? Did Jesus connect his mission and the creation of the church? If he did, how did he link the two? And did the early church pick up that cue and develop it, or was it lost in subsequent preoccupation with the being and atoning work of Christ?

To use the language of current Christological debates, ecumenical and Mennonite, we begin with Christology from below. We begin with the historical Jesus and with the mission of this Jesus. We begin there because that is where the early church began. Christological reflection in the New Testament is a function of explaining the meaning of the words and deeds of the historical Jesus to Christian churches in diverse pastoral situations. Early Christian Christological thinking is a response to improper thinking or morality in the church or missiological issues facing the church. Church leaders, trying to address these problems, point to the life and work of Christ. Christological reflection, narrowly defined, is a function of interpreting the mission of the historical Jesus.

Jesus and the church

We begin with Jesus and ask: Do we have any indication in the Gospel accounts of Jesus' life and mission that picture him as the convener of the church?

We select two texts where Jesus speaks of the church. Space does not permit us to look at others that would be helpful, e.g., Luke 4:16-30 and its use of Isaiah 61.

Matthew 16:17-19

> Blessed are you, Simon Bar-Jona,
> for flesh and blood has not revealed this to you
> but my heavenly Father.

And I say to you: You are Peter
and on this rock I will build my church
and the gates of Hades shall not prevail against it.

I will give you the keys of the reign of heaven
and whatever you bind on earth heaven shall bind
and whatever you loose on earth heaven shall
loose.

The context of this saying is a discussion about the question, Who is Jesus? The issue is identity and mission. Who are you? What is your mission? The question concerns Christology.

Jesus answers the question by saying, "You are correct, I am the Messiah. I am the fulfillment of the scriptural and Jewish peoples' hopes for the messianic figure of the end time. As the Messiah my mission is to build the church on the rock."[8]

The rock is a powerful image in Judaism. It is the sacred point of contact between heaven and earth from the time of Jacob's dream in Genesis 28. The rock is eschatologized in the prophets. It becomes the holy mount, the navel of the world, the sanctuary of the nations (Isa. 2:2-4; 60; Jer. 3:17; Zeph. 3; Zech. 8). In the intertestamental and early rabbinic writings, the rock becomes the place where God is especially present in history to be with, to protect, and to save his people.

Jesus' messianic mission is to build the church on the rock. The word for church that Jesus uses is *ecclesia*. This term is used in the Old Testament to describe the gathered assembly of God's people. It is the end-time community of salvation in the Dead Sea Scrolls. Jesus' messianic mission is to gather the end-time people of God on the rock, to gather them together into the presence of God so that he may save and protect them.

This text brings together two classic messianic themes, the cosmic rock and the messianic building. The Messiah

8. Marcus Borg, *Conflict, Holiness and Politics in the Teachings of Jesus*; A. E. Harvey, *Jesus and the Constraints of History*; Gerhard Lohfink, *Jesus and Community*; B. F. Meyer, *The Aims of Jesus*; E. P. Sanders, *Jesus and Judaism*; John Riches, *Jesus and the Transformation of Judaism*.

in Judaism is expected to build a new temple, a new creation, where God will dwell in a new and powerful way among his people. Jesus says that his mission is to build the church on the rock as that messianic building. Jesus' mission is to gather the people of God together into the church as the visible community of God's presence in the world. The church is the place where the coming of God into the world is most clearly evident. The church is where the kingdom of God is most visible.

Jesus says two things about the church on the rock. First, the church will triumph over the gates of Hades. The phrase "the gates of Hades" is used in the intertestamental literature as a synonym for Satan. That is, Satan and the powers of the demonic will not break through the defenses of the church that is built on the rock. Jesus builds the church with the promise that the presence and power of God is greater than the presence and power of the demonic.

Secondly, the church "binds and looses." Binding and loosing is technical language that means two things. 1) It is used in intertestamental literature to mean the binding of Satan and the loosing of people bound by demonic powers. The language is used this way in the New Testament. (See Mark 3:27; 7:34-35; Matt. 12:29; Luke 13:16; Rev. 20.) To bind and to loose means to overcome Satan and to liberate victims from demonic powers. 2) To bind and to loose also means to engage in ethical discernment about what is right and/or wrong, to bind and to loose behavior consistent or inconsistent with the law, to judge or forgive where disobedience has or has not occurred.

Binding and loosing in Matthew 16 is clearly a reference to the binding and loosing of Satan. It is defined by the church triumphing over Satan and by the keys of the kingdom. The image of keys is associated with the binding of Satan in Revelation 20.

Jesus builds the church on the rock as a kingdom outpost to bind the powers of the demonic in the world, and to liberate people from demonic powers and structures. The church is the kingdom community where Satan is bound and where people are loosed.

Binding and loosing in Matthew 18 defines the church as a
community of ethical discernment. The church is to bind
and loose the way Christians live in the world. When a
brother/sister sins she/he is to be bound or loosed, confronted about the sin and called to repentance or loosed from
the perception of having sinned. Where repentance does
not occur, the church is to discipline. This understanding of
binding and loosing is also the meaning of the John 20:23
reference to binding and loosing associated with the gift of
the Holy Spirit. Christians who have the Spirit are to
engage in ethical discernment, forgiveness, and discipline.

Jesus builds the church as a kingdom outpost of ethical
discernment. The church is the gathered people of God discerning what it means to live as the people of God in the
world, and to hold each other accountable to the consensus
discerned.

Jesus' mission

Jesus came preaching the kingdom of God, the eschatological presence of God in kingly power and rule. He defines
his primary kingdom mission as the gathering of God's
end-time people to build the church as the visible sign of
the kingdom.

That is a startling definition of Jesus' messianic mission. His mission is ecclesiological; it is to build the church.

Do we have other clues in the Gospel accounts that
might point the same direction? I suggest five other signs
that indicate a similar interpretation for the mission of
Jesus. Space does not permit a detailed analysis of these
signs.

First, Jesus chose twelve disciples (Mark 3:14-16).
Jesus' action symbolized his mission to restore the twelve-
tribe people expected of the Messiah and end-time salvation. The lost sheep of Israel in Matthew 10:6 is the entire
people of Israel, not isolated Jews. It is the lost sheep of
Ezekiel 34. The appointment of the twelve was a symbolic
prophetic action; it announced the eschatological gathering
of the people of God.

Secondly, Jesus healed people. We do not grasp the meaning of Jesus' healing activity if we understand the miracles as performed primarily for individuals. Jesus interprets his healing ministry in terms of Isaiah's prophecies of the restoration of God's people (Matt. 11:5; Luke 7:22). In the eschatological people of God, all must be made whole.

Thirdly, Jesus taught the disciples to pray at their request (Luke 11:2), teaching them the disciples' prayer (Lord's Prayer). To have a distinctive prayer was an essential mark of identity for religious groups in Jesus' time. The prayer defines the disciples as a community. The content of the prayer intensifies that understanding. The address, "Father" (*abba*), is a term of intimacy and immediacy. Fathers create families, communities of identity and security. The next phrase, "sanctify your name," is a reference to Ezekiel 36. The name of God has been desecrated by the dispersal of his people in the world. God, the prophet says, will gather and renew his people in the last days. It is God, not we, who sanctify his name, and he does that by re-creating his people. The next phrase, "your kingdom come," is parallel to the first. It is precisely in God's gathering of his end-time people that the kingdom of God comes. It shines forth in the people of God.

Fourthly, Jesus interprets the meaning of his death in peoplehood terms. The vicarious death of Jesus establishes a new covenant. The death for the *many* serves to reconstitute the covenant relationship between God and his people that was shattered by sin and disobedience. The death of Jesus fulfills the promises of God to make a new covenant, to create a new people that will live in a new, free, and open relationship with God.

Fifthly, Jesus speaks constantly of a new people of God that he is gathering. He does so with a wealth of corporate pictures: the flock, the throng of wedding guests, God's planting, the net, God's building, the city of God, the members of the new covenant.

Jesus defines his kingdom mission as the gathering of a renewed community of God's people, as the building of the church. The kingdom of God requires a people of God. No kingdom, no people; no people, no kingdom. Jesus' mis-

41

sion is to gather the end-time people of God through whom God reigns in kingly power.

All Jews knew that. They could not think of the Messiah or the kingdom of God apart from peoplehood. The problem was that they thought of this peoplehood in nationalist terms. It would be for Jews only. Jesus' mission to regather the people of God breaks the bounds of this nationalism with a universal vision. The nations are going to sit at the messianic banquet with Abraham, Isaac, and Jacob (Matt. 8:11).

Jesus' mission was to establish the rule of God in visible form. The shape of that visibility was the church. God's eschatological presence and rule is present in the world in a concrete people. Jesus' mission was to build the church on the rock as the community where God is visibly present in history to bind and to loose.

Jesus defines his mission in ecclesiological categories; he is the convener of the church.

Moving beyond Jesus

What happened to Jesus' ecclesiological definition of his mission in the early church and in the writings of the New Testament? Is the relationship between Jesus' mission of building the church and Christological reflection retained, or even expanded, or is it lost? The remainder of this paper argues that Christology is defined ecclesiologically in the writings of the New Testament. Space does not permit a detailed exposition of the linkage. What follows is an identification of key components of the Christological-ecclesiological linkage that need further expansion and testing.

The work of Christ

The New Testament writers assert that "Christ died for our sins." The theological meaning of this affirmation is not explained definitionally or dogmatically, i.e., Christ died to satisfy the wrath of God, or Christ died to demonstrate the love of God. Rather, the meaning of Christ's death is interpreted through a variety of different metaphors: expiation, ransom, reconciliation, freedom, righteousness, adoption, new creation, life, victory over the powers, sacrifice (at least seventeen different images). No single term is capable of wholly explaining the meaning of Christ's death. The multiplicity of images used to interpret the meaning of Christ's death suggests that Christ rescues from whatever the human predicament is. The work of Christ meets a remarkable range of different human needs and sins. To proclaim the saving work of Christ did not mean for the early Christians proclaiming one particular transaction, but meeting the vast variety of needs felt by people in different situations. The meaning of Christ's work was interpreted in such a way that it could be adapted to different cultural, social, and personal contexts.

Atonement creates a people

The metaphors used to interpret the saving work of Christ are centered by two themes that run through the images. The first is that the saving work of Christ creates a people. The language used in the New Testament to interpret the work of Christ is Old Testament covenant and peoplehood language. A brief comment on some of the key terms will illustrate the point.

Suffering and sacrifice language is Old Testament covenantal and kingly language. It is, first of all, covenant language associated with the Passover and the making of the covenant. The sacrifice of the lamb at Passover is a communal event that creates a community. The lamb is slain for the family. The four Gospels and Paul (1 Cor. 5:7; 11:23-26) interpret the death of Christ as a Passover event. The Passover sacrifice creates a new covenant and a new covenant community.

Suffering and sacrifice language in Isaiah also becomes kingly language. The suffering servant suffers and gives his life as a sacrifice. But a reversal of values and roles takes place. The suffering servant becomes the king. All the kings of the earth bow down before the servant become king. The suffering and sacrifice of Jesus in the New Testament is interpreted as the enthronement of the messianic king. And the king is the king of a people. To become king via suffering is to create a people.

Suffering and sacrifice language in the New Testament
is not fundamentally concerned with satisfaction ideology,
but with covenant peoplehood theology. God is renewing
his covenant through the death of Jesus to regather his
end-time people, to build the church.

Expiation has similar connotations. To expiate means
to cleanse and to cover. An expiatory sacrifice is one that
purifies and covers sin, and thus mediates forgiveness. The
context of expiation is always the community of God's people. Sin has collective consequences; it injures and breaks
relationships. Expiation and forgiveness cover or heal the
injury and thus restore relationships. Disturbed relationships in the community of God's people can be restored
through the provisions of expiation.

The death of Jesus is an expiatory sacrifice. The classic
text is Romans 3:23-26 (quoted in structural outline form):

> **A** for *all have sinned* and fallen short of the glory *of*
> *God*
> > **B** *being made righteous* freely
> > > **C** *by his* grace
> > > > **D** through the redemption
> > > > > **E** the one in *Christ Jesus*
> > > > > **E** *whom* God purposed
> > > > **D** an expiatory sacrifice through faithfulness
> > > **C** by means *of his* blood
> > **B** to prove his *righteousness*
> **A** through the passing over of before having happened
> *sins* in the forbearance *of God*
> to prove his righteousness in the now time,
> to be himself righteous even making righteous out of
> the faithfulness of Jesus.

God purposed Christ as an expiatory sacrifice for the purpose of redemption. The means of the sacrifice for redemption is the faithfulness of Jesus as demonstrated by his
death on the cross (by means of his blood). The purpose of
the expiatory sacrifice is to demonstrate the righteousness
of God in passing over previous sins because of his forbear-
ance. The words *pass over* and *restraint* are not positive
words which describe God's forgiveness or even neutral
words that picture God as simply disregarding sin. Rather,

44

they are negative words in Judaism. The problem is God's inactivity, his failure to act in behalf of his people. The language points to outsiders. God's patience with the sins of the Gentiles, the sins of Israel's oppressors, is the problem. The Jews fear that patience allows those sins to go unpunished (Isa. 42:14; 63:15; 64:10-12; Ps. of Sol.; 4 Ezra; 2 Bar., 2 Macc. 6:14). This fear reflects a widespread tradition in which God's patience is conceived negatively as self-restraint which allows the sins of the Gentiles to accumulate.

The presentation of Christ as God's expiatory sacrifice asserts that God has now acted justly with the previous sins of the Gentiles which he had passed over due to his patience. Christ is God's means of expiation for the Gentiles. For the first time they too have access to an expiation, as the Jews have had for generations through the sacrificial system. God purposed Christ as a means of expiation in order to make right his relationship to the Gentiles as well as their relationship to the Jews. God has healed injured relationships by means of expiation, and made possible genuine community between enemies. A community of Jews and Gentiles is possible because God has cleansed the sin.[9]

If we turn to another major atonement category, *righteousness*, we discover a similar emphasis. Righteousness is Old Testament covenant language. It is concerned with covenant behavior, with loyalty to the covenant relationship to God and within the community. It speaks of faithfulness in covenant relationships. The concern is the right ordering of the world according to God's intention. The model of righteousness is God. He is the righteous one. His righteousness is his fulfillment of the demands of the covenant relationship, and the restoration of persons deprived of the covenant relationship.

Righteousness language in Paul, the primary user of this terminology, refers to the eschatological faithfulness of God to his covenant and promises to save all humanity, especially the Gentiles. Paul's concern is the eschatological

---

9. John E. Toews, *Romans*, unpublished manuscript, Believers Church Commentary Series.

ordering of the cosmos according to the covenant and the promises to Abraham. The context for Paul's use of righteousness language is Jew/Gentile relations in the church, especially the legitimacy of Gentiles as equal partners with Jews in the new eschatological community God is creating in the world in Jesus Christ (Romans and Galatians). The means of the revelation of the righteousness of God is the faithfulness of Jesus. The question being answered by righteousness language is how God keeps faith with himself to include the Gentiles in the people of God.[10]

Reconciliation is peoplehood terminology. In four of the five uses of reconciliation language in Paul (the only New Testament writer to use the word), the concern is the creation of a new peoplehood. In 2 Corinthians 5:17 the point of reconciliation is a new creation, a new social phenomenon, in which old realities are replaced by new realities. Reconciliation in Ephesians 2:14-16 concerns the creation of "one new humanity" of Jews and Gentiles in which both are reconciled to God. Colossians 1:20 pictures a reconciliation of all created reality to God through the cross of Christ. Colossians 3 identifies specifically Jews and Gentiles as the objects of the reconciliation. Reconciliation language in the New Testament concerns the reconciliation of alienated peoples to God and to each other, the creation of one new people out of two peoples.

The work of Christ also means *adoption* into a family. The image is a family metaphor. The family is the people of God. The saving work of Christ incorporates non-family members into the family. It creates genuine community out of alienated and lonely people.

Redemption, or purchase, language also comes from the Old Testament. It is exodus-redemption language. Redemption is primarily collective. God redeems a people. He purchases them from slavery to one set of masters to be his own possession. The same nuance is carried over into the New Testament. To picture the work of Christ as redeeming or purchasing from sin denotes primarily a change of ownership. In Romans 6, the change is from slaves of sin to

10. John E. Toews, *Romans*, unpublished manuscript, Believers Church Commentary Series.

slaves of righteousness. First Corinthians 6:19 makes the point that Christians are not their own but the possession of Christ. The transfer is from the rule of darkness to the kingdom of God's Son in Colossians 1:13. In Acts 20:28, the church is the possession of God "which he purchased with the blood of his own." To redeem or ransom is to create a people under lordship.

Only six atonement metaphors have been examined. But they are among the more central in the church's atonement theology. All concern the creation of a people. The saving work of Christ is first and foremost a peoplehood creating work. "Christ died for our sins" to create a people, to build the church, to convene the church.

Atonement is cosmic

The second theme that runs through and unifies the atonement metaphors is that the saving work of Christ has cosmic proportions. The predicament from which Christ rescues is not simply a personal, or even a communal, one. It is a cosmic crisis. There exists a cosmic estrangement that involves all people and all created reality. The whole creation groans and travails. The groaning and travailing are the birth pangs of a new creation which is already taking place in Christ and the church. The saving work of Christ is transfer from slavery to the ways and powers of this world to the transforming ways of Christ and the power of the Spirit.

New Testament atonement theology outlines the consequences of this transfer of allegiance in the context of the church. It does so with the profound conviction that the down payment of the Spirit is already a renewing and transforming reality. In Christ, a new creation, a new endtime reality, is emerging.

This cosmic transformation theme is a very important one. Traditional atonement theology is too individualistic and too moralistic. The problem in the world is not primarily individual wrong choices, but the power of sin, the total corruption of sin as power which makes holiness and relationships in community impossible. Total pollution and destructiveness lie at the core of the old order. The inter-

pretation of the saving work of Christ as the creation of a
new order based on a totally different charter (covenant), a
new creation empowered by the Spirit, produces the pro-
foundest challenge to the human and cosmic realities of
sin. The saving work of Christ is most fundamentally the
reality of God coming to right the wrongs of a flawed creation, the corruption of the total order of reality—natural
and social, moral and religious, personal and structural—
with a new world order. The foretaste and the sign of that
new world order is the church.

Driver suggests that Ephesians, especially 2:11-22,
offers the clearest statement of New Testament atonement
theology.[11] I agree with him, but make the point more radically yet. Ephesians 1 concludes with a prayer for the
church. The final petition is for the power of God that made
Jesus prime minister. God is the subject of verses 20-22.
He has raised Jesus from the dead and made him prime
minister (to be seated at the right hand in the ancient
world means to be made the prime minister). Paul is
describing an event in God's world politics. He is picturing
the victory and establishment of the kingdom of God. The
political event announced is the enthronement of Christ.
This enthronement takes place at the expense of all the
powers. God has made Jesus the prime minister of the
world, of all the powers, in the resurrection and exaltation.
God has effected a change of government in the universe.
The extent of Christ's prime ministership is indicated in
verse 22: all things, all cosmic reality, have been put under
his feet.

The subject changes suddenly in verse 23, and against
the rules of grammar. God was subject. Now the church is
the subject. A writer changes the rules of grammar to
make a significant point. The point is that God has made
Jesus prime minister and head over all things *for the
church*. And the church as subject is defined as the body of
Christ and the fullness of Christ.

Body language in the Bible is public language. The
body is the public manifestation of a person. The church is

---

11. John Driver, *Understanding the Atonement for the Mission of the Church,*
213ff.

the public manifestation of Christ, the prime minister. The church also is the fullness of Christ. The language comes from the Old Testament concept of *shekina*, the glorious presence of God that fills the tabernacle or temple. It is the dynamic means by which God demonstrates his presence among his people and to the world. The church is the *shekina* of Christ. It is the means of Christ's full presence in and for the world.

Ephesians 2 describes the birth of the church. Jesus, the prime minister, creates a new people out of two peoples. This new people, "one new humanity" (v. 15), is the public manifestation of the *shekina* of the prime minister of the universe.

The relationship is profoundly dialectic. Christ is exalted by God as the prime minister of the universe *for the church*. The purpose of God's work in Christ is the church. The church in turn is a new reality purposed to reveal the nature and reality of Christ, the prime minister. God in Christ is creating a people, the church, which is to manifest the reality and mission of Christ in and for the world.[12]

Christ defines his messianic mission as the building of the church on the rock. The New Testament interprets the saving work of Christ as the gathering of the people of God, as the creation of a people, as the building of the church. The purpose of Christ's saving work is the church. Christ is the convener of the church.

The identity of Christ

So far we have focused on the question of Jesus' messianic mission and the work of Christ. What about the identity of Christ? Or, to state the question in more traditional language, what about the nature of Christ? Does the debate about the person of Christ have anything to do with the church or with Christ as the convener of the church? Much of the debate about the nature of Christ has not linked Christology and the church. If the assumptions of the debate are challenged, however, the question regarding the nature of Christ is related to the nature of the church.

12. Markus Barth, *Ephesians*, vol. 1, 145ff.

The debate concerning the nature of Christ has historically been anchored at two points, the titles of Christ and the preexistence or incarnation texts. The debate about the meaning of the titles has centered on the divine/human question and the evolutionary or developmental question: the questions of early versus late, or development from within versus the accretion of ideas from outside. This form of the debate is a function of later Christological agenda shaping the way Christians read the New Testament. It would not have occurred to first-century Jewish Christians, e.g., Paul, Matthew, John, to think in those terms. They interpreted the meaning of Christ in terms of Old Testament and Jewish categories.

The titles are attempts to interpret the meaning of Jesus' mission and person in the light of Jewish Scriptures and traditions. The central issue is always peoplehood. Terms such as Messiah, Lord, Son of Man, and Son of God, for example, are all concerned with peoplehood. The Jews expected a Messiah to liberate Jewish peoplehood from oppression and to inaugurate the long awaited messianic kingdom. The language of the lordship of Yahweh which is transferred to Jesus in the New Testament is concerned with Jesus' function as Yahweh to save, protect, and form the people of God in a world of evil and demonic powers. The issue at stake is the power of God over evil and demonic realities, not the being of God. The Son of Man is a collective term from the beginning. Jews and most Christian scholars agree that in Daniel it is a reference to the people of God. Only over time is the referent individualized. But then it is clear that the individual Son of Man represents and fulfills the mission of Israel. Jesus, as the Son of Man, is fundamentally concerned with the judgment and salvation of a people. The Son of God title in the Old Testament refers to Israel. In the intertestamental literature, Son of God becomes linked with the Messiah. The Son of God is another term for the Messiah who comes to save and liberate the people of God. At no point in Judaism or the early church does either Son of Man or Son of God connote the humanity or divinity of Jesus, as in the later Christological debates.

The same is true with other Christological categories in

the New Testament. To describe Christ as the pioneer (Acts 3:15; 5:30-31; Heb. 2:9-10; 12:2) is to picture him as the captain of a people. He is the leader of a people who shows his people how to live. The way to follow the pioneer in Hebrews is through the obedience which Jesus manifested in his life. Or, to present Christ as the firstborn is to define him as the first of his people. It is an Old Testament term that shows God's claim on his people, on all those who follow after the firstborn. Paul correctly defines Christ as "the firstborn among many brethren" (Rom. 8:29). He is the first of God's new people.

But certainly, it is argued, Christ as new or second Adam contrasts the divinity of Christ with the humanity of Adam. Adam was human and sinned. Christ was divine and sinless. Therefore, Christ replaced Adam. That reading of the Adam-Christ typology is possible only by ignoring a whole body of reflection on Adam in Jewish intertestamental literature. Adam is pictured in two different ways. One interpretation is that Adam is the cause and explanation of sin (the traditional Christian way of reading the Adam reference in Rom. 5:12-21). The second exalts Adam as the first Israelite. In this interpretation, Adam is regarded as the first patriarch. His lineage is transmitted to Abraham through Shem and Seth. He is the first of Israel's race. Adam is created circumcised; he is the first Jew. Adam is pious; he does what Israel is to do later. Adam is a high priest dressed in the garments of the high priest; he makes sacrifice. Adam is a type of Moses. Moses' staff, created on the sixth day, is handed from Adam to Moses. Abraham, Isaac, and Jacob are buried with Adam in the cave of Machpelah. In this interpretation, Israel is the main purpose of God's creation. Israel is no longer God's attempt to create an alternative to sin in the world, but the original creative purpose of God. Adam is the image of humanity God intended in creation, a humanity to be restored in the eschatological age. Sin is ascribed to other causes: Eve, Satan, the angels mingling with women (Gen. 6).

This interpretation of Adam as the first Jewish patriarch theologizes that Israel is God's true humanity which will overcome the power of sin in the world. The last Adam is eschatological Israel. In other words, this version of

Adam theology advances a claim about the place of Israel in the purposes of God. During the Maccabean period, this Adam theology gets transposed into a nationalist theology. Israel alone is God's true humanity to undo the power of sin. Adam, as an eschatological type, is a reference to national Israel.

We completely miss the radicality of Paul's theology in Romans 5 if we fail to read verses 12-21 without the benefit of this background. Paul introduces a revolutionary argument. The role assigned to Israel has been taken by Messiah Jesus. The role the Jews gave to Israel, Paul gives to Christ. Israel and the law are not the answers to the power of sin, but the faithfulness of Messiah Jesus. Christ is the last Adam, not Israel. Christ alone can liberate humanity from the power of sin.

That is why the answer to the problem of sin is baptism into Christ, not the law (Rom. 6). Baptism into Christ means baptism into the people of whom he is the head, not primarily initiation into a personal relationship with Christ. Just as "baptism into Moses in the cloud and the sea" (1 Cor. 10:2) refers to incorporation into the people of whom Moses is the leader, so baptism into Christ refers to incorporation into the people or body of which he is the head.

The agenda in the Adam-Christ discussion is the role of Christ vis-a-vis Israel. Christ replaces Israel as the means of God's salvation of a people. He brings Israel's mission to fulfillment, and offers salvation to the world, and he now extends Israel's mission to the world by incorporating the nations into the people of God.

The preexistent or incarnation texts—Jesus is the Son of God made flesh (John, Paul, Hebrews, 1 Peter)— describe how the Son of God became human rather than how a particular human being, Jesus, became the Son of God. While the divine sonship of Jesus theme in these texts is important to establish his role as the representative of God, it is not the central point of these texts. The central point is that Jesus is the representative of God to create a people of God in the world. The Gospel of John, which has the clearest incarnational theology, makes it clear that the function of the incarnate Christ is to form a people who will be faithful to God (John 17).

I hope my point is clear. The fundamental concern of
New Testament Christology as reflection on the person of
Christ is peoplehood formation. The mission of Christ as
Messiah, Savior, Lord, Son of God, firstborn, new Adam,
image of God, and Word become flesh is the regathering
and renewal of the people of God, and the incorporation
into that people of peoples from all nations.

From the side of the church

So far we have looked at the Christology-ecclesiology linkage from the side of Christology. A study of the linkage
from the side of the church would be equally illuminating.
Space does not permit more than an allusion to the fruits
of such a study. Many metaphors are used in the New Testament to bond the church to Christ: the body of Christ,
members of Christ, the head of the church, the body of this
head, the growth of the body, the fullness of God, the bride
of Christ, a letter from Christ. The different images all
speak of one reality: the church of Jesus Christ. The
metaphors all have a common referent: Jesus Christ. They
point beyond themselves to the people Christ is creating in
the world. Jesus is the creator, the convener, of the church.
(See Toews, 1989, for the development of this point.)

Convener of the church

I have made the case in this paper that Jesus defined his
messianic mission as the building of the church on the
rock, and that New Testament Christological reflection on
the meaning of Jesus' work and identity consistently links
Christological interpretation with the formation of the people of God. New Testament Christology is concerned
with ecclesiology, with the gathering of the end-time people
of God in the world. The central thesis of New Testament
Christology is that Jesus is the convener of the church.

New Testament ecclesiology makes the same point
from the side of the church. The central thesis of New Testament ecclesiology is that the church is called into existence by Jesus. He is the convener of the church.

So what? What is the meaning for the Mennonite

churches that Christ is the convener of the church? I suggest several things. First of all, we are challenged to interpret Christ's saving work in ecclesiological categories rather than individualistic terms. While Christ does save, redeem, reconcile, and adopt individual pagan men and women, the central concern of New Testament Christology is building the church. Jesus' mission is the church. He or she who has no people, no church, has no Savior and no Lord. She or he who confesses Jesus as Savior and Lord is part of his people. There is no salvation without the church. New Testament Christology calls us to build the church theologically and sociologically as our fundamental passion. We dare not be seduced by the modern heresy of individualism. Mennonite ecclesiology was theologically and sociologically correct even if not explicitly anchored Christologically. The challenge facing Mennonite churches is to recover and expand our historic theology of the church as an authentic discipling and disciplining community. That recovery and reshaping will require a genuine spiritual renewal and empowerment because all the forces of our culture move us away from such a theology and sociology. To the extent that we can recover and reshape, we also will be more effective in our missionary activity in the modern world. A gospel that saves individuals but does not incorporate them into authentic church communities is no gospel and does not save. Only a gospel that calls people to profound repentance and change and incorporates them into communities of accountability and mutual responsibility is grounded in a Christology that is biblical.

Secondly, we are challenged to formulate a Christology that is genuinely biblical and that answers the theological and missiological questions of our time as the classical creeds did in their time. Some of the critical issues facing us are different than in the fourth century. Therefore, our formulations will be different than in the classical creeds. If one of the pervasive heresies of our time is individualism, if the fruit of that individualism is anomie, and if Christ is the convener of the church, then we will need to formulate a Christology that speaks about Christ as the kind of person who builds authentic community, about Christ as a whole person who heals the fracturedness of modern individuals and integrates them into communities of centeredness, healing, and meaning.

The late modern and post-modern world is a creative time for Christological thinking, as were the third and fourth centuries. We must encourage our teachers, pastors, and missionaries to think and test new Christological thoughts. One component of this theologizing should be to develop more systematically and carefully the Mennonite intuitive Christology that Christ is the convener of the church. That is a Christology which I have argued is biblical and contemporary.

Christology: discipleship and ethics

Harry Huebner

Patristic Christologies rooted in Nicea and Chalcedon have dominated the thinking about Jesus in Christendom. The central question has been: How can Jesus simultaneously be human and of the same metaphysical stuff as God? Regardless of the specific answers, beginning the Christological discussion this way has had serious implications for discipleship ethics. Since it meant that for humans to be like Jesus required them to take on divine essence, and since this was considered to be heretical, it was seldom thought that discipleship could be the moral linkage between Jesus and us. After all, we cannot be like Jesus precisely because Jesus was divine and we are not.

While the divinization debate may have dominated Christological discussions, there have been other ways of speaking about Jesus. For the early church and for others like the radical reformers much later, "who Jesus is" was first of all understood to be an ethical question, i.e., what is the moral character of Jesus? This led them to see that they could not claim the significance of Jesus for themselves without simultaneously committing themselves to follow after him. This is not to say that they did not address metaphysical issues, nor that these were unimportant for them, but they found it difficult to speak about who Jesus was without speaking about his character as normative for them.

John H. Yoder has summarized for us many specific

ways mainline Christian ethicists have found of declaring Jesus irrelevant in constructing their ethic. They are:

1. Jesus' ethic was intended for a brief interim just prior to the passing of this world;

2. Jesus was a simple rural figure not relevant for complex societies like ours;

3. Jesus lived in a world over which he had no control;

4. Jesus' message was spiritual and not ethical;

5. Jesus was a radical monotheist and this relativizes all human values;

6. Jesus' mission was to give his life for our sins.[1]

Each of these is an explanation of why discipleship cannot be the language of Christian ethics.

Although the specifics are different, the irrelevance-of-Jesus arguments have led to similar conclusions regarding the church. The church has simply not been conceived of as a moral category. Ethicists have not found ways of speaking about it as a moral agent, nor as a moral training ground, nor even convincingly as the moral authority. The church as body of Christ can only be properly understood once Jesus as the way of God for all nations is made intelligible. What underlies our efforts in this study is the inclusion of both Jesus and the church in the formation of a Christian ethic. I want to examine what is meant by claiming that Jesus is fully normative. There are two components to this examination: First, what does the character of Jesus tell us about who we are? Second, what does it tell us about who God is? Another way of asking the question is: What are the moral implications of the Chalcedonian affirmation that Jesus is fully God and fully human?

Learning to be like Jesus

Obviously we cannot sort through the many entanglements of the historical Jesus debate in this short study. Nor is it necessary. Although we agree with many of the insights this debate has generated, nevertheless, our

1. *The Politics of Jesus* (Grand Rapids: Eerdmans, 1972), pp. 16-19.

approach is different. They assume that the picture we have of Jesus in the Gospels is a reflection of the theology of the early church. So far we agree. They conclude from this that therefore the accounts themselves are not reliable and hence irrelevant for an accurate reconstruction of Jesus. Here we disagree. The difference between us is not so much a hermeneutical difference as it is an ecclesiological one. Our assumption is that it is precisely because these are accounts by the church that they can be trusted—not necessarily as verbatim detailed accounts, but trusted to embody the truth of God for people like ourselves who also want to be the church. If it were not for the stories of the early church, we could not know the character of Jesus.

The character of Jesus

Already in the birth narratives, we get a glimpse into who this one who is being announced is. Announced to an unwed mother, he is born to lowly people in a lowly place, from Nazareth and not Jerusalem, and although his father is in the Davidic kingship line he is nevertheless not really his father. It should not be surprising then that he was not recognized as king by many people apart from the lowly. From the very beginning it appears that the Gospels want to introduce the coming of the Christ child as being *for* the underlings of history.

Luke does not keep us in suspense long on the kind of reign that is being envisioned. It is spoken of in explicitly social and ethical categories in the songs of Mary and Zechariah. The one whose birth is being proclaimed is one who will be a radical social transformer: the mighty will be put down from their thrones and the lowly will be exalted, the hungry will be filled and the rich sent away empty, the people will be saved from their enemies, knowledge of salvation will be given and forgiveness of sins will be received (Luke 1). And later when Jesus makes his first public appearance in Nazareth, he confirms this platform by reading from Isaiah 61. Here the poor, the captives, the blind, and the oppressed are singled out as the recipients of good news (Luke 4:18). And in the Sermon, again the poor,

58

the hungry, the ones who weep, and the hated are pro-
nounced blessed. Woes go to the rich, the satiated, the
happy, and those well spoken of (Luke 6). Here Jesus gets
specific regarding his expectations of his followers. What
he identifies as essential is that we be loving and merciful
—but in a way so radical that it extends to enemies that
strike us and steal from us.

The compassion which Jesus showed for all who are
caught in the power of sin and oppression, whether this be
structural or personal, is something that spans his entire
ministry. Whether it be the many healings; his teaching
about the new way of peace, love, and justice; his confrontation of the religious leaders; the feeding of the multitudes; the many exorcisms; the confrontation with truth of
those who seek or doubt; his lamentation over Jerusalem;
or his willingness to face death rather than confront his
enemies with violence: the identity of Jesus is so tied up
with setting others free from the power of sin and evil, that
he truly came to be seen as the man for others.

The way of Jesus

Sometimes Christians think that in knowing the object of
Jesus' concern, we know who Jesus is and how we can be
like him. All we then need to do is be similarly concerned
and opposed to these things. But nothing is further from
the truth. In fact, *what* Jesus is opposed to is not what
makes him particularly different from the way the
prophets were understood. *The way* he opposes these
things seems new to most of his hearers.

This way gradually becomes clear as the story unfolds.
At first, ensuring that everyone has enough to eat commends itself as the way to bring about justice and salvation. And although Jesus feeds the multitudes on occasions during his ministry, nevertheless "we do not live by
bread alone." Bread is an important part of the new kingdom, but it does not fully define the way. Perhaps then the
new kingdom can be ushered in through the political structures already in place. This commends itself as a way of
getting to all the nations quickly. But Jesus also rejects
this way, not because all nations should not hear about it,

nor because his is not a relevant message for the governments of the nations, but because it cannot be heard from a position of dominance.

The third way presented to Jesus is to incarnate the love of God without getting involved in the bitter consequences that flow from living this way. The temptation is for Jesus to proclaim this radical message and yet stay clean himself. But Jesus also rejects this temptation, not because there is some strange benefit derived from "getting your hands dirty," but because proclaiming a way of life without living it yourself has no integrity. None of these ways are adequate to the way of salvation embodied by Jesus.

Jesus chooses a different way. He selects a few followers and embarks on the process of being a godly person in their midst and teaching them a new message of love, forgiveness, and shalom. This group of people is to carry on the incarnation of Immanuel by themselves being the presence of God among the people in a manner like Jesus.

While Jesus was with this group of disciples, he taught them how to see God: how to recognize the salvation of the Lord. One of the things he taught was perhaps the hardest lesson for us all to learn, namely, about the consequences of being messengers of truth in a world of sin, i.e., about the cross.

The way of the cross is hard for us to understand. So was it for the first disciples. I remind you of the discussion that took place at Caesarea Philippi. When Jesus asked his disciples whether they knew who he was, and when Peter answered correctly that he was the Son of the living God, then Jesus assumed that Peter knew what he had said. So he proceeded to remind them of what it means to be the representative of *agape* in a hostile and sinful world. That when love meets sin, love gets hurt. When he lays this before his disciples, hoping that they will understand, he is disappointed. Peter, who had correctly answered the "Messiah question" just a few minutes earlier, now vows to protect Jesus with violence. And so Jesus challenges him to open his eyes and look again. Then Jesus makes it explicit and personal, and says, "If anyone would come after me, he must deny himself and take up his cross daily and follow me" (Luke 9:23). Our way is often the way of violence; God's way is the way of the cross.

This is not some strange morbid imagery which the disciples could not understand. Jesus is saying concretely that when we act from the standpoint of power and dominance, from control and violence, then God cannot become present in this world. God can only become visible through those who incarnate the sacrificial love, compassion, and forgiveness of God, only through those who themselves put on the very character of God. To do this in the presence of sin and evil, however, may be costly. Yet, on the other hand, it is the only hope of radically undermining the destructive power of evil.

The cross is not an event which stands for every kind of suffering, however. It is the concrete historical reality which expresses sin's penultimate triumph over its radical confrontation with God's truth. (It is, of course, not an ultimate triumph.) In a world of sin, the cross is inevitable.

The cross, like Jesus' entire life, does not suggest passive acceptance of suffering. It is one of the clearest confrontation of the fraudulent power of sin. As the writer of Colossians puts it, when explaining what Jesus did on the cross, "He disarmed the principalities and powers and made a public example of them, triumphing over them in him" (Col. 2:15).

Walter Wink, an American biblical scholar, has recently argued that the traditional passive interpretations of the Matthean account of turning the other cheek, walking the second mile, and giving your cloak to someone who takes your coat, are inaccurate. For example, to turn the left cheek to someone who strikes you on the right (Matt. 5:39) is an act of defiance towards one who is treating you as an inferior. It is a direct challenge to the person to treat you as an equal, as a fellow human being. Only inferiors are slapped on the right cheek with the back of the hand. When you turn the other cheek, you are in effect saying, "Try again. I deny you the power to humiliate me."[2]

The way of Jesus is the way of the cross. Not because

2. Walter Wink, *Violence and Nonviolence in South Africa: Jesus's Third Way* (Philadelphia: New Society Pub., 1987), p.16.

61

Jesus was a masochist, but because he was *agape* incarnate. Love wills to redeem sin through forgiveness, love confronts patiently with the truth, love is present to pain with compassion. Sin cannot tolerate such love. It wills to destroy it, for if it does not, then sin itself is devoured.

Being like Jesus

The Gospels, as well as the Epistles, are explicit on how we ought to be like Jesus. Passages like Mark 10:42-43, John 15:12, 2 Corinthians 5:15, Galatians 5:24, 1 John 4:12, and others, have led John H. Yoder to conclude that:

> There is thus but one realm in which the concept of imitation holds—but there it holds in every strand of the New Testament literature and all the more strikingly by virtue of the absence of parallels in other realms: this is at the point of the concrete social meaning of the cross in its relation to enmity and power. Servanthood replaces dominion, forgiveness absorbs hostility. Thus—and only thus—are we bound by New Testament thought to "be like Jesus."[3]

Being like Jesus, therefore, does not entail taking on divine essence, nor is it mere passive imitation or robotic repetition. It entails putting on his character by putting on like virtues. Yet mere mimicking of virtues is not what is involved here either. We need to become virtuous like Jesus himself was virtuous. This is not a simple matter. It requires becoming part of a community whose very preoccupation is to learn to become the body of Christ.

Learning to be a servant community

In our society, ethics has become an intensely personal and private matter. We do not permit ourselves to tell each other what kind of people we ought to be. In fact, terms like *ought* and *ought not, right* and *wrong, good* and *bad* have almost all become taboo. We tend to believe that we do what is right insofar as we act freely. When things are my choice, then they are right; when not, then, since I am being coerced, they cannot be right.

3. *Politics*, p.134.

62

Discipleship ethics is incompatible with such an excessive individualism, and instead is rooted in a social reality. This is so because it is premised on the belief that we are called to be a particular kind of people, God's people. Therefore, as Stanley Hauerwas puts it, ". . .the first words about the Christian life are about a life together, not about the individual."4

This view of ethics makes several assumptions. First, that ethics is inherently communitarian. Discipleship ethics acknowledges that our identities are shaped by the communities in which we live and that what we do flows from who we are. Furthermore, it sees the quest for autonomy as itself a basic denial of the possibility of Christian ethics.

Second, it acknowledges that who we are is a gift we have received from others and is not first of all a self-creation. Like any gift, we have the power to accept or reject it, but when we reject it, we can only turn to a different community to embrace another gift.

Third, that there is no such thing as an unqualified ethic. Ethics, as such, does not exist. There is only *Christian* ethics, *utilitarian* ethics, *Jewish* ethics. That is, ethics requires a community for it to have content. Communities are always concrete. In this respect, ethics is like a language. You cannot just speak. You must speak either French or English or German.

Fourth, discipleship ethics is not written from the perspective of the masses. Rather, it is written from the perspective of those who have opened themselves to formation by the God of Jesus Christ. God is the moral authority. Hence, it cannot be a minimalistic or democratic ethic.

Fifth, Christian ethics presupposes a distinction between church and world. This does not suggest that the distinction is between realms of reality which God has ordained, e.g., between orders of creation and redemption, between private and public spheres, or between the withdrawn and the non-sectarian, and that each realm properly requires a different ethic. The distinction is not rooted

---

4. *The Peaceable Kingdom: A Primer in Christian Ethics* (Notre Dame: University of Notre Dame Press, 1983) p.97.

in the character of God at all, but rather in the character of humanity. It is between those who claim to be his disciples and those who do not.

Discipleship as learning

Another word for *disciple* is *pupil*. Originally the word was used to designate someone who was attached to a master, to learn what the master knew, to learn to speak the language and think the thoughts of the master, do what the master did, and to become like the master in all respects. This enabled disciples to carry on the tradition or even the life of the master.

Learning as disciples learn is not unfamiliar to us. Consider, for example, how, as a child, you learned to be good, or how you teach children to be good. Parents know that this kind of learning takes place by imitation and repetition. So they try to get children to apologize when they have done something wrong or to return a toy that has been unfairly taken from another child. Parents try to get their child to repeat patterns of behavior in the hope that it will become part of the child's character. They try to *disciple* the child to become good. It is indeed sad, however, when the child performs the desired behavior only in the parent's presence. When this happens, we say that the child has not really learned to be good. Although the child has heard, s/he has not appropriated what has been heard.

This example tells us something about how we learn to be good. Two things are involved: first, the process of becoming aware of the good—this usually happens through hearing and/or seeing others; second, the process of claiming what you hear/see as your own. The relationship between these two is admittedly complex and can more adequately be described in the unmechanistic language of socialization than in terms of cause and effect. We really do not know why it is that some can hear/see constantly and not appropriate, while others have hardly ever heard/ seen and yet have somehow appropriated the good. We do know that we become good persons insofar as we make the virtues of a community our own.

The process of appropriating moral virtues obviously

does not happen all at once. It requires careful and pro-
longed training, much like the process athletes engage in.
For example, if we do not conscientiously train ourselves to
be hopeful, we will not be; if we do not train ourselves to be
patient, we will not be. Contrary to what we often think,
these are not mere personality givens. For Christians, the
training is, however, also unlike athletes in that it is neither individualistic nor competitive. Learning Christian
moral skills takes place in the Christian family called
church.

Christian moral character training comes from hearing
the Word of the Lord together with others. *Fides ex auditus*, a dictum of the Latin church, which literally means
"faith comes from hearing," also applies to ethics. We learn
who we are by hearing it from others whom we trust. The
speaking which enables such hearing to take place is a special kind of speaking—one which encourages its hearers to
claim what is being heard, precisely because it is the Word
of *life*. Such speaking is an invitation to make *the* story
our story.

Making the story our story

The church does not exist first of all because it is our creation; it exists because God has called people together and
is trying to mold them into a community which reflects the
love of God to the world around it. That is, God becomes
known through the incarnational activities of God's people.
Who God is, is seen through divine acts via God's faithful.
We cannot know God apart from this because the epistemology of God is concretely social.

Often our tendency is to think that in order for the
church to be relevant to society, we must downplay our
Christian distinctiveness. We ask, How can we effectively
engage in dialogue with our neighbors if we do not speak
their language? We tend to think that it is precisely in our
identification with, and not our distinction from, others
that we can help them understand what being Christian is
all about? This logic leads to an appeal to general principles of epistemology like nature or God, which transcend
Jesus and promote the understanding of ourselves in our

sameness with those who do not claim to be disciples of Jesus.

This is the very thing we want to reject. The church is where the story of Jesus is told and becomes alive. The church is where the story of Jesus becomes the story of a real historic people. The church is that body which strives to adopt the character of the good Samaritan, and the forgiving father in the prodigal son story, and the story of the cross, as its own. While the church is morally distinct from the world, it is always radically present in it.

This view of church has several specific implications for how we view ethics. First, as we concretely make this story our own, we cannot accept the injustices around us—poverty, violence, hunger, greed, selfishness, sexism—without hope that the transforming power of God is still at work; without the patience to care even though our actions seem ineffective; without the compulsion to speak the truth in love, even within earshot of those around us who will find such language threatening because of their complicity with an oppressive status quo; without the love that binds us to needy people in our lives who take far too much time and energy away from our otherwise important preoccupations.

Second, the agenda for the church is not set by the world around us, but by the story of Jesus which the church claims as its own. The central theme of this story, which is now our story, is the cross. Becoming people of the cross is therefore the central concern for the Christian church. The danger, however, is that this remain an abstraction. We need to work hard at incarnating the love of God in Christ Jesus in that part of the world where our lives are lived. We need to work hard at living our lives there where the lowly are, and in solidarity with them. While the focus of our identity is lodged in the content of the story which is given to us, this story is never really *for* us. The main theme of our story is best understood via the paradigm of the gift of love: the more we give, the more we receive.

Third, our story therefore comes with specific content. It is not an empty form for us to fill according to our own best insights. The story tells us that we cannot call ourselves Christian unless we work daily at making love, hope, joy, patience, kindness, goodness, faithfulness, gentleness, self-control, humility, forgiveness, charity, servanthood our virtues. These are the Christian virtues that give content and direction to our moral lives as the servant community.

Fourth, this model intentionally shifts the moral focus away from decision making, toward being the church of Jesus Christ. Of course, decisions are always being made. However, for our model, the process begins at a different point. The first, and most important question we must ask is, Who are we? The answer for us Christians is given by the content of the story we have claimed. Second, What is going on? The answer to this is given by intensive social and historical analysis. And the third, What must we do and how can we find the courage to do it? All three of these are the function of the church community being itself.

Fifth, when this process is put to work, one of the things that happens is that the moral issue itself gets reinterpreted. Permit me one example. We sometimes think that we are forced to choose between saying divorce is wrong, thereby implying that the married persons must suffer their difficulties, and saying that in this particular case divorce is permissible, thereby depreciating the importance of marriage. Faced with this dilemma, we are often inclined to abandon all attempts to be ethical and simply give pastoral support. Our approach begins at a quite different point. We realize that how the matter is put already tells us something about what we think about ourselves. We say that in conscientiously working at becoming people who believe in the way of Christ—in hope, redemption, and the possibility of transformations—we are able to believe in new beginnings. To counsel that marriages do not need to break up is not a callous disregard for the pain of people in a broken relationship, but is grounded in the belief that God is actively at work in this world healing broken relationships. Such faith may well restore what earlier seemed hopeless.

Sixth, worship is the most profound moral act. The process of remembering who we are gives shape to the

identity of the church as the moral community. In worship
the people gather to remind themselves that they are people under God. It has sometimes been thought that an
emphasis on spirituality/worship was in tension with
Christian ethics. After all, spirituality is an exercise which
invites God to act, whereas Christian ethics focuses on the
importance of who we are and what we do. True spirituali-
ty/worship has to do with opening up our lives for the possibility of God acting through us. True spirituality/worship
is therefore not in tension with Christian ethics at all. To
be in harmony with the way of Jesus is to be in harmony
with the spirit of God.

Becoming God's people

Earlier we stated that our examination would have two
parts. So far we have dealt only with the entailments of
the claim that Jesus is fully normative for us. Now we
want to ask what implications the claim that Jesus is the
full revelation of God has for ethics.

I want to begin by pondering the legitimacy of the distinction between conceiving ourselves as followers of Jesus
and conceiving ourselves as people of God. There is a danger for discipleship churches to cling to the former at the
expense of the latter. For example, the Anabaptist/Menno-
nite tradition has told us that we are to do what is com-
manded by God through Jesus, although God reserves pre-
rogatives which may emanate from a different character.
The way of Jesus is the way of love and forgiveness—the
cross—but the way of God may well be the way of the
sword.

Clearly, this is problematic, First, such a fractured
view of God, which can simultaneously legitimate both the
cross and the sword as ways of dealing with sin, results in
appalling Christological consequences. Are we to believe
that the way of Jesus is, in the final analysis, not the way
of God? Or are we to believe that he is only a partial revelation, i.e., of the good side of God? Neither view is acceptable, especially for the discipleship tradition where following Jesus is credible only since he is "fully God and fully
human." Second, this view of God leads inevitably to a

68

dualistic ethic which legitimates being like Jesus on some occasions and like violent God on others.

This theological dualism has generated such thorny problems for serious thinkers that few, since Augustine, have escaped its contradictory implications. The attempt by Anabaptist/Mennonites to circumvent this difficulty by saying that God is not normative for us, only Jesus is, tends to lead to the belief that we can and must participate in violence: if God resorts to such means in the final analysis, then surely it must be necessary. God's way shows us that there is some metaphysical necessity to ultimately resort to an uncross-like manner in dealing with sin, and that the crosslike way is but for a few, to remind us of the good side of God. Insofar as we really want to take sin seriously, the argument continues, we have no other alternative but to resort to uncrosslike means.

I want to make the bold suggestion in conclusion that Jesus is the full revelation of God. This is not to say that every true statement about Jesus can, without error, be attributed to God, or vice versa, but that the full character of God comes into clear focus in the character of Jesus Christ. Stated simply, the way Jesus deals with sin—the cross—is the way God deals with sin.

This suggestion cuts across our problem in a new way. Although it is clearly not without its theological problems, it nevertheless deals with the most basic of all challenges to the relevance-of-Jesus-for-ethics claim, namely, that if Jesus is only a partial revelation of God, then he is only sometimes normative for us. God as warrior, as angry judge, and as destroyer of the evildoer is also normative for us precisely because the ultimate necessity of God's resorting to violence (I assume all would claim this as a last resort, even for God) implies the ultimate inadequacy of the nonviolent way of the cross.

God as sufferer

It follows from what we have said that the traditional view of God as one who cannot suffer because of God's perfection is untenable. If Jesus is the full revelation of God, then the perfection of God is given content via the cross of Christ.

Then we can no longer construct a God-concept with a pre-conceived notion of perfection. Perfection now means the willingness to suffer death in order to save sinners. The invitation to be perfect as our heavenly Father is perfect now takes on new meaning.

The cross is then no longer seen as a contractual arrangement between Father and Son for the appeasement of an angry Father. The cross is precisely God's way of dealing with sin. That is, God's becoming present among us sinners, in lowliness and suffering, in God's full *agape* is the ultimate way in which the power of sin can be vanquished.[5] What we see in the cross event is precisely God at work reconciling the world while bearing the curse of sin. All the biblical injunctions to follow after Jesus in his suffering are in fact calls to go into the world's places of injustice and there embody the love of God.

What this means ethically is that now we as followers, who are called to be concerned about undermining the power of evil in the world, can participate with God in a whole new way of life. Rather than confronting evil with threats or acts of violence, our weapon is the word of truth which states that violence, indeed all evil, is not the last word. Since God's way is the way of suffering in response to evil, we now know that this is the way evil will eventually be redeemed. We now know that love is more basic than hatred, and accepting suffering more redemptive than causing suffering. We now know that the love of God in Christ Jesus really reigns. We now know that God did not simply instruct Jesus to perform a specific task, but that in Christ Jesus the truth of God is disclosed.

Since we know that the same God who lovingly redeemed us from the power of our sin is the one who wills to do the same for all, it becomes possible for us as follow-ers to believe that the truthful way to confront evil, all evil, is to participate in the patient *agape* of God. Moreover, the motivation for doing so is no longer the command of one who may well resort to other means in a crunch, but the

---

5. For a helpful study of this theme see C. Norman Kraus, *Jesus Christ our Lord: Christology from a Disciple's Perspective* (Scottdale: Herald Press, 1987).

binding power of love which is the true source of life. We can now no longer make the distinction between how God deals with sin among the redeemed and how God deals with sin in the world. We can no longer believe that big sins or serious sins are dealt with in one way, whereas little sins can be dealt with via forgiveness. Invitation and forgiveness are but the logical extension of the grace of God. The word of God to all sin is forgiveness. The word of God to all sinners is: you are forgiven, come and follow the way of abundant life.

This means that with boldness we can speak the truth that God's love reigns. This same word is spoken to all: to the disobedient child and to the murderer; to the superpower leader and to the church college president; to the pregnant teenager and to the married couple in difficulty; to the main street poor and to the suburban rich; to people of the first world and to people of the other worlds; to homosexuals and to heterosexuals. *What* we say is not determined by who we are saying it to, but by who we are. Although there may well be different methods of speaking, because not all hear with equal ease, there is but one answer to the problem of sin and evil; God's nonviolent cross.

God as judge

Contrary to what some might think, this view does not deny the judgment of God. Rather it understands judgment in the context of the full normativeness and revelation of Jesus. Here judgment is not rooted in the violence of God, but emanates from the invitational nature of God's truth. It is possible to reject the call of God, but in so doing we reject the way that leads to life and salvation. Hence, we choose death. But death is never willed by God. The incarnation teaches us the very opposite, namely, that God is willing to suffer even death in order to save us from destruction. This is different from saying that God is an angry judge who willfully destroys people who have been given a fair chance, yet do not accept. God wills passionately that all people come to salvation. Yet God's love is invitation, not coercion.

God as Savior

The God of Jesus Christ wills to save us and all the people of this earth. The story tells us that this salvation does not come via dominion, neither God's over us nor ours over anyone else, but rather through God's patient presence among us, lovingly releasing people from bondage. Becoming people of God, becoming the body of Christ, means that we say yes to the invitation to put on like character and similarly to will to become present to the suffering people of this world; that we train ourselves in the courage necessary to endure the pain of speaking the truth to the destructive powers around us. Anything short of this is not to follow Jesus the Christ. However, in doing this we must train ourselves to resist the inevitable temptation that comes from being moderns, namely to think that we are masters of our own fate. This temptation can be overcome by collectively opening ourselves to the only power that can and will transform our own hostilities and divisions into a whole new reality. Then we can embrace the joy of the Seer in Revelation that the Lamb that was slain, contrary to what most are able to believe, is the meaning and driving force of history. And then we can challenge all to follow him.

Be the church of Jesus Christ

Our North American society teaches us daily that we are to take charge of our lives, be strong, independent, know what it is that we want to achieve and then go achieve it. Many non-Christians around us tell us that they look in vain for real differences between us and them. The world outside of this continent, whether Christian or not, sees our church as being in complicity with the imperialistic and self-seeking goals of our governments. Discipleship ethics challenges this.

The verdict is not yet in whether the North American church, or more specifically, the North American Mennonite church, will be able to convince the larger world of the integrity of its faith. We will only be able to do this by living as moral people, and by calling the people of our own nation to live the ethic of Jesus which reflects the character of God. The next revolution in North America may well be a moral revolution. The church as the moral community can, by being the church of Jesus Christ, provide leadership and impetus for it. It also may not. May the merciful God of patience and truth grant us wisdom and courage to be God's faithful people.

How central the cross?
Response to "Christology: Discipleship and Ethics"

Mary H. Schertz

Let me first express my gratitude to you, Harry, as well as to the others who have contributed to this conference. The points you have opened for discussion are important ones, ones which the church needs to address carefully if the gospel of Jesus is to continue to make sense to Christians in our times.

As an initial response to what Harry Huebner has accomplished here, I want to summarize what I perceive to be the two major thrusts of his paper and, in the course of that summarization, to do some evaluation and to raise some questions.

I have found it helpful to think of this paper as promoting two kinds of agenda. On the one hand, Huebner is proposing a process for doing Christian ethics that differs in some major ways with the way Christian ethics has frequently been done. That proposal in itself merits our serious attention. On the other hand, he is suggesting a content or a criterion for that process of Christian ethics. This content is based on a theology of the cross. That proposal, too, merits serious attention.

On the subject of doing Christian ethics, Huebner implicitly rejects some more traditional approaches in which the ethicist debates, from abstract philosophical principles, such questions as: Who is the good person? What is the just act? The more traditional approaches, whether argued deontologically, teleologically, or from the point of view of response ethics, often concluded that Jesus is irrelevant to the ethical inquiry. Huebner rejects that conclusion and declares boldly that Jesus is fully normative for Christian ethics.

Narrative approach to Christian ethics

Keeping that declaration central, Huebner goes on to suggest that a narrative approach to Christian ethics has a greater possibility of maintaining the normativity of Jesus than the more traditional approaches. This narrative approach to Christian ethics involves two basic steps. First, the church which God has called together claims the story of Jesus as its own. Secondly, the church reenacts the story. It incarnates the story. It embodies the story. These two acts of claiming and reenacting the story of Jesus involve a number of activities: telling the story in congregations of believers; doing acts of justice-making; experiencing cross-bearing and solidarity with the lowly; loving each other; worshiping. In thus claiming the story and living our lives in accordance with it, we extend the story. The stories of the life of the church become analogous to the story of Jesus. These stories are perceived as *types* of the story of Jesus. These stories improvise, in infinite variety, upon the core story of Jesus. The fundamental questions of ethical inquiry then are not what constitutes the good person or the just act on an abstract or theoretical level. The questions of ethical inquiry have to do with whether the stories of the church correspond to the story of Jesus in significant ways.

Huebner's proposal is an attractive way to think about Christian ethics from a variety of perspectives. It is attractive from the perspective of biblical theology because the language of the Gospels is not, for the most part, abstract, philosophical language which lends itself readily to traditional ethical inquiry. The language of the Gospels is concrete and metaphorical. It is story language. Therefore, Huebner's proposal accommodates the language of the Gospels more readily than some of the more traditional approaches to Christian ethics.

This proposal is also attractive from a pastoral perspective. First, it is probable that the stories which we hear and with which we live have a more profound and powerful influence over our attitudes and behaviors than philosophical arguments and theses. One of our recent seminary graduates, after several terms with Mennonite Central Committee in Nicaragua, spent some time trying to explain Central American justice issues to North American Mennonite congregations. People who were unmoved by statistics and logical arguments were transformed and motivated to costly action on behalf of Central America when she began telling the stories of the people.

Secondly, from a pastoral perspective, the proposal puts the tasks of ethical inquiry back into the hands of congregations. Ethical reflection upon stories, the stories of Jesus and the stories of the church, is a task in which believers, from teens to great-grandparents, can take part.

Finally, this proposal is theologically attractive as well. It does what John Toews has suggested. It keeps the concepts of Christ and the church closely and vitally connected. From the point of view of the proposal, we cannot consider the story of Jesus without considering the stories of the church—and vice versa.

Need for conceptual language

As attractive as the proposal is, however, it soon becomes clear that narrative ethical inquiry also needs to make use of more abstract and conceptual language. We need this kind of language in order to think about and to talk about whether and how the stories of our lives correspond to the story of Jesus. Again, Huebner implicitly acknowledges this need for the abstract by suggesting that the theme of the cross is the criterion by which we judge how well we are living in accord with the story of Jesus.

It is at this point of the selection of the theme of the cross as *the* criterion of narrative ethical assessment that I am troubled by a lack of rationale or argument for the selection. While I find Huebner's description of the cross moving and eloquent, the basis of its selection remains unclear.

Huebner says, "The central theme of this story, which

is now our story, is the cross. Becoming people of the cross is therefore the central concern for the Christian church."

It is not immediately apparent that the claim of the centrality of the cross emerges from either the biblical story of Jesus *or* from the stories of the Mennonite churches.

The biblical source upon which Huebner relies most heavily is the Gospel of Luke. While the cross is important to Luke, it is, I think, clearly secondary to the theme of proclamation, the preached word. Luke must be read in continuity with the Old Testament and Acts. When so read, it is clear that there is continuity between the word of the prophets, Jesus' proclamation of the kingdom, and the disciples' preaching about the death and resurrection of Jesus. In each case, there is suffering and the cross is experienced. However, while the death of Christ is atoning, the suffering of the disciples is almost incidental. The emphasis is the gospel message not the suffering that usually, but not always, accompanies it. If the cross as central theme of discipleship does not emerge clearly from Luke, how and why *is* the selection valid?

In the case of the Mennonite story, it is at least arguable whether we see ourselves as people of the cross or not. In my congregation, we told stories this spring. These stories were analogous to the story of Jesus in that they involved motifs of ministry, identification with the lowly, suffering, and redemption. But, although the cross figured heavily in some of these stories, we understood ourselves to be telling stories of what it means to be an *Easter* people, not primarily people of the cross.

Additionally, in seminary, I learned that a Mennonite Christology, a Mennonite telling of the Jesus story, should include: the life and ministry of Jesus; his death and resurrection; his exaltation and his identity as the second person of the trinity. A Mennonite Christology, we decided, would specifically *not* emphasize one of these motifs to the exclusion of the others.

Of course, a series of congregational stories and a seminary class discussion do not disprove Huebner's selection of the cross as central theme. These examples do, however, indicate that Huebner's elevation of the cross as central does not represent either a consensus of New Testament scholarship or a consensus of Mennonite experience. My point is not that the cross is an inappropriate selection. Huebner is actually fairly convincing in his development of the theme's implications for discipleship and ethics. There may be good reasons for this emphasis. My point is only that the criterion for assessing the correspondences between the story of Jesus and the stories of our lives ought to be clearly argued instead of assumed.

In conclusion, I think both proposals are exciting contributions to this study. I would encourage careful discussion of both. What possibilities do Huebner's proposal of narrative ethics have for Mennonite theology and church life? What is the central theme of the Jesus story? Is it the cross? How? Why? If the cross *is* the most significant theme for us to emphasize in our time, how do we make the case? If the resurrection is also significant for us to emphasize in our time, how do we make the case? If a more holistic emphasis on the life and ministry of Jesus as well as his death and resurrection is important to emphasize, how do we make the case?

The way of life embodied by Jesus

Response to "How Central the Cross?"

Harry Huebner

I thank Mary Schertz for a thoughtful response to my
paper. She is correct in identifying areas in my paper
which need further discussion and clarification.

I begin with a brief clarification of my use of the term
cross. By cross, I do not simply mean the event of the cru-
cifixion, i.e., the death of Jesus or even merely the suffering of Jesus. I speak rather of the cross as symbol of a way
of life embodied by Jesus which resulted in his defenseless
death. This way comes into clear focus in his response to
sin—his willingness to give a loving, healing response to
people caught in the powers of destructiveness. This is the
manner in which I take Jesus to be using the term when he
says to his disciples "Take up your cross daily and follow
me" (Luke 9:23) and "Whoever does not bear his own cross
and come with me, cannot be my disciple" (Luke 14:27).

Not only am I contending this as the biblical meaning
of the cross, I take it to be morally and theologically significant to speak of it in this manner.

First, it points to the costs of discipleship. Such a way
of life is not patterned after a concern for self-defense.
This specific moral life resulted in Jesus' death. Compassion, love, and forgiveness have this quality—in focusing
on the welfare of the other they risk loss of life. The stories
of the Good Samaritan, the Prodigal Son, the Kingdom
Parables, as well as many stories in the Old Testament,

such as Abraham, Isaac, Jacob, Joseph, Moses, Ruth, can all be read as stories of the cross, in that they take part in a way of life based on love's graciousness and gentleness.

Second, to designate this way of life as the way of the cross points to the ultimate truth of its moral content. Not even the threat of death can falsify the virtues embodied in the life of Jesus. The power of their inherent moral truth transcends this threat. The goodness of this life is commended to all as something worth dying for.

Third, if discipleship is not given moral content via the death of Jesus, then it cannot be a moral metaphor for pacifists. Or, to say it differently, unless discipleship is rooted in the cross, self-defense and the justification of violence remain the moral preoccupation of the church.

Resurrection linked to cross

It follows directly from my usage of cross that resurrection and cross are essentially linked. Yet we must remember what the resurrection confirmed—namely, the nonviolent life of Jesus. The resurrection, apart from the cross, cannot be of any moral relevance to Christians, because in itself it has no content. The resurrection alone only symbolizes the victory of God. Until we establish what it hails as victorious, it remains a contentless triumphalism, a view all too familiar in contemporary society. Jesus does not ask his disciples to take up the resurrection and follow. That would be meaningless; firstly, because it is not ours to take up—it is God's gracious blessing bestowed upon us—and secondly, it identifies no content for blessing. The resurrection alone cannot therefore be a basis for a Christian ethic. By inviting his disciples to the way of the cross, there is an implicit promise that although there may well be suffering and pain involved, this is, nevertheless, the way of true victorious living because it is based on the truth of God. The godly cannot remain dead even though they lose their lives. Hence, as the resurrection without the cross is contentless, the cross without the resurrection is but a morbid story.

I therefore find the dichotomy implicitly presupposed in Schertz's way of stating the critique, namely, between an

Easter people and a people of the cross, problematic. I
readily accept the criticism that my paper was not explicit
enough, perhaps not even clear enough, in spelling out the
relationship of cross and resurrection (tight editorial
restrictions prevent one from saying all) but I do not accept
that it projects a view of the cross apart from resurrection.
Repeatedly, it emphasizes the importance of seeing the
transforming power (resurrection) inherent in the embodi-
ment of this life by the faithful community. (See, e.g., my
reference to divorce.) In fact, this is the central thesis of
my paper. The whole effort to root the life of Christ in the
character of God is an attempt to establish the claim that
the way which took Jesus to the cross is the way of God.
Since it would be nonsensical to suggest that the way of
God is the way of death, Jesus' way of the cross becomes
the way of life. If this claim can be sustained, then it
establishes the cross/resurrection connection with a radi-
calness not often stated. That is to say, not only is Jesus'
death on the cross morally significant for us in that it
demonstrates the ultimacy of his commitment to the peace-
making virtues over his desire to save his own skin, but it
is precisely God's resurrection of Jesus that demonstrates
the ultimate moral truth of this way of life. Hence, the resurrection confirms the way of Jesus as the way of God.
The life of God—true life itself—is not a life different from
the one which led Jesus to the cross, but the same. And
that is why Jesus was raised from the dead.

When the virtues inherent in the narrative of Jesus are
seen simultaneously as the virtues of God and the virtues
of disciples, then it follows that to be a people of the cross
is to be an Easter people. To say it any other way violates
the possibility of rooting a Christian ethic in discipleship.
What, after all, could be the motivation/rationale for
embracing a way of life which entails denial of self-interest
or even the acceptance of death, except the faith and
promise that this is the way of salvation? And how can
this be said more powerfully than to claim continuity
between Jesus' way of life with God's? Might it be, therefore, that those who read my paper as failing to give proper
emphasis to the resurrection do so because they are
uncomfortable with the extremely tight linkage I, in fact,

maintain between cross and resurrection? Might it be that they desire a good life not quite as costly as that symbolized by the cross, and believe that concentration on the resurrection might let them off the hook? If anything, it seemed to me as I reread my paper, that I might have overstated the case for the linkage between cross and resurrection, even though it is true that the word resurrection never appears in the paper.

I also see it as problematic for Schertz to dichotomize the theme of proclamation in Luke with the theme of the cross. Can the Lucan kerygma really be given other content than the new life in Christ Jesus symbolized by his altruistic self-surrender in *agape* to others (the cross)? Can the good news be understood in any other way than as an identification of this way of life with the victorious life? Has the church really ever accepted anything less? The moral implications of this claim have no doubt been thoroughly disputed—and that is the debate which my paper attempts to engage in—but the former I am prepared to assume.

Christology in historical perspective

J. Denny Weaver

Christology, defined narrowly as the study of the nature
and person of Christ, occupied the center of the theological
stage for the first five centuries of Christian history. The
issues of Christology stand at the heart of any comprehen-
sive theological undertaking, regardless of the tradition
doing the theologizing. The radical reformation of the sixteenth century constitutes one of the roots of the modern
believers' church tradition, and Mennonites are modern
heirs to the Anabaptist part of the radical movement.
These movements—in fact all of Protestantism—came into
existence nearly a millennium after the fixing of the traditional terminology of Christology. While it is quite appropriate and necessary that these rather late-appearing
Protestant groups deal with Christology, less obvious is
why they should presume to have something unique to say
on the subject. In fact, theologians belonging to all the
Protestant traditions have argued that the relative new-
ness of Protestants in general and of the believers' church-
Mennonite tradition in particular—a bit more than 450
years in contrast to nearly 2,000 years—gives the newcom-
ers little new to say on Christology and even less right to
say it to the world at large.

This essay argues the opposite point, namely, that
because of its unique place in history, the believers' church
tradition, to which Mennonites belong as charter members,
does—or at least can—have a unique perspective on Chris-

tology. In making that argument, the various believers' church traditions might appear the most audacious of all the Protestant groups. However, the historical niche in which Anabaptists and Mennonites find themselves does much to explain why they and other believers' church people should pursue the Christological questions rather than simply accepting unreservedly the time-honored tradition.

At their origins in the Protestant Reformation of the sixteenth century, Anabaptists endured persecution and rejection not only from Catholicism but also from what became majority Protestantism. A number of titles distinguish Anabaptists from other components of the Protestant Reformation: Radical Reformation, Left Wing of the Reformation, Third Reformation, Anabaptist Reformation. While these names have differing emphases and connotations, together they clearly underscore the idea that the Anabaptists from whom Mennonites are descended were not merely Protestants. The title of Walter Klaassen's little book quite properly described them as "neither Catholic nor Protestant."[1] In light of this history of standing over against both mainline Protestantism as well as Catholicism, it seems appropriate to ask whether Anabaptists and Mennonites have, or ought to have, a perspective on Christology different from majority Protestantism or Catholicism. In fact, one might more appropriately be surprised if that separate historical identity did not stimulate any unique insight or perspectives into Christology. In this paper, we will explore some questions which the Anabaptist-Mennonite location in history raises about the traditional theological formulas. As a preliminary to that discussion, the following section outlines the position with which believers' church theology is in dialogue. Subsequent sections then indicate believers' church perspectives through an analysis of the historical development of the church's language on Christology as well as by using several examples from early Anabaptist history.

Although this essay speaks about Christology for Mennonites, understanding and/or accepting the analysis

1. Walter Klaassen, *Anabaptism: Neither Catholic nor Protestant* (Waterloo, Ont.: Conrad Press, 1973).

does not depend on prior identification with a particular Mennonite subculture. Most properly speaking, this essay treats Christology from a believers' church perspective. As such, it assumes a non-Constantinian stance (explained below) in its use of the biblical data and its analysis of historical developments.

The formation of the creeds

A received tradition supplies the framework and the vocabulary from within which much of the Christian church discusses Christology. Formulas which emerged from the church councils meeting at Nicea in A.D. 325, and at Chalcedon in A.D. 451, embody that time-honored outlook.

The statement authorized by the assembly at Nicea reads:

> We believe in one God the Father All-sovereign, maker of all things visible and invisible;
> And in one Lord Jesus Christ, the Son of God, begotten of the Father, only-begotten, that is, of the substance of the Father, God of Gods, Light of Light, true God of true God, begotten not made, of one substance with the Father, through whom all things were made, things in heaven and things on earth; who for us men and for our salvation came down and was made flesh, and became man, suffered, and rose on the third day, ascended into the heavens, is coming to judge living and dead.
> And in the Holy Spirit.[2]

A later council repeated this formula almost verbatim and incorporated it into what Christians now call the Nicene Creed.

In ordinary language, the Nicene formula affirms the deity of Jesus. While that impulse appears at several instances, the key phrase is "of one substance with the Father." It states that Jesus and the Father are of the same substance, essence, or being. The technical term for this way of describing Jesus is *ontological*, that is, having to do with his being. In other words, the Nicene formula

---

2. The statement concludes with a list of terms judged unacceptable, and anathematizes any person who accept them. The translation cited here is from Henry Bettenson, ed., *Documents of the Christian Church*, 2nd ed., (London: Oxford, 1963), p. 25.

identifies Jesus ontologically, in terms of essence, substance, or being.

With this formula, the church fathers at Nicea intended to secure the divine origin of salvation. By saying that Jesus' being was God's being, the origin and control of salvation by God was certain.

In the aftermath of Nicea, the Trinitarian language familiar to us became formalized. Its principal architects were the three Cappadocian Fathers, Gregory of Nyssa; his older brother, Basil of Caesarea; and Gregory Nazianzus. They addressed the questions of monotheism and the person of Christ: How can one equate Jesus with God the Father without either affirming the existence of more than one God or undercutting the high claim about Jesus? How can one defend the unity of the Godhead while simultaneously making a distinction among the ways of being of the one God? The Cappadocians used a language of threeness to say that while God in his essence and being is one, he has three persons, with Jesus as the second of the three persons. God the Father is the first person of the Trinity while the Holy Spirit is the third. The doctrine of the Trinity thus developed as a formula with which to say that the Godhead was one (thus preserving monotheism), while at the same time distinguishing three different personages or ways of being—three persons—within the Godhead.

More than a century after the Council of Nicea, the Council of Chalcedon, meeting in A.D. 451, articulated a formula which constitutes another part of the familiar, received tradition of Christology. The definition of Chalcedon reads:

> Therefore, following the holy Fathers, we all with one accord teach men to acknowledge one and the same Son, our Lord Jesus Christ, at once complete in Godhead and complete in manhood, truly God and truly man, consisting also of a reasonable soul and body; of one substance with the Father as regards his Godhead, and at the same time of one substance with us as regards his manhood; like us in all respects, apart from sin; as regards his Godhead, begotten of the Father before the ages, but yet as regards his manhood begotten, for us men and for our salvation, of Mary the Virgin, the Godbearer; one and the same Christ, Son, Lord, Only-begotten, recognized in two natures, without confusion, without

change, without division, without separation; the distinction of natures being in no way annulled by the union, but rather the characteristics of each nature being preserved and coming together to form one person and subsistence, not as parted or separated into two persons, but one and the same Son and Only-begotten God the Word, Lord Jesus Christ; even as the prophets from earliest times spoke of him, and our Lord Jesus Christ himself taught us, and the creed of the Fathers has handed down to us.[3]

In ordinary language, this definition purportedly affirms the humanity of Christ.

First, we should note that this statement reaffirms the language from Nicea which says that Jesus was one substance with the Father. However, exclusive attention to the divine nature of Jesus can overshadow Jesus as a human being. Chalcedon's goal was to hold the two themes of deity and humanity together. Thus after reaffirming Nicea's definition of deity, the operative phrases in Chalcedon's definition are those which affirm Jesus as one substance with us in his manhood, and those which state that the human nature and the divine nature can be neither separated nor fused—they are "without confusion, without change, without division, without separation; the distinction of natures being in no way annulled by the union, but rather the characteristics of each nature being preserved and coming together to form one person and subsistence, not as parted or separated into two persons, but one and the same Son and Only-begotten God the Word, Lord Jesus Christ."

Through the phrases used, the authors sought to reconcile the emphases of two competing theological schools, those of Alexandria and Antioch. Alexandria thought it more important to underscore the unity of Jesus' person. Thus they said that in the incarnation, the Word became *flesh.* The other, Antioch, thought it more important to stress the distinction between human and divine natures. They spoke of incarnation in terms of Word becoming *man.* The counterbalancing phrases in the Chalcedonian formula, stressing now unity of Jesus' person, now distinction of two

3. Bettenson, *Documents*, pp. 51-52.

natures, reflect the concerns of the two schools of Antioch and Alexandria.

Nicea and Chalcedon in historical reflection

This section of the chapter seeks to examine these definitions from Nicea and Chalcedon in historical perspective. First, we need to acknowledge the distance between the death of Christ and the final statement by Chalcedon. That distance spans approximately four and one-quarter centuries. It is twice as far from Jesus' death to Chalcedon as it is from the American Revolution to our own time. Depending on the age of the reader of this manuscript, the time from Jesus to Chalcedon is about the same as the time from the origins of Protestantism and Anabaptism in the sixteenth century to the time of our parents or grandparents. Using another kind of comparison, by the time Chalcedon arrived, more than one-fifth of the Christian history we know had elapsed.

Distance in time certainly does not in and of itself render a statement problematic or untrue. However, languages and cultures do change over time. The distance between Jesus' death and Chalcedon then should lend a note of caution against making the precise words of Chalcedon the criterion by which to measure whether or not one has read the New Testament correctly. In other words, while historical distance does not falsify these definitions, that historical distance can help us to understand how there might be some other possible and correct ways to talk about the nature and identity of Jesus.

Second, with awareness of the historical distance in mind, what developments in the more than four centuries from the death of Jesus to the Council of Chalcedon are important for consideration of Christology in believers' church perspective? One way to answer is to describe the themes debated in those passing centuries. The definitions at Nicea, by the Cappadocians, and at Chalcedon were answers to questions posed but left without specific answers in the New Testament. One question concerned the relationship of Jesus to God. Already in the Gospels, but more so in the theological letters, the New Testament writers used language about Jesus which they also applied to God. However, the biblical writers did not explain how to do that without violating the principle of monotheism. Nicea and the Cappadocians were attempts to resolve that tension which exists in the New Testament. A second question concerned the nature of Jesus. Alongside the New Testament texts which use God language about Jesus, the New Testament writers are also very clear about the fact that Jesus was a historical person, a human being. The New Testament does not resolve the tension between identifying Jesus with both human life and divine being. Chalcedon's definition attempted to speak to that tension.[4]

In the time from the end of the New Testament to Chalcedon, there was a great deal of theological discussion and debate about Christology. Along the way, the theologians of the church rejected a number of answers to the New Testament's questions, in part because the answers had an unsatisfactory balance of one or the other of the poles involved.[5] The definitions given by Nicea and the Cappadocians and Chalcedon were accepted by the power structures of the church and then enforced by them as the correct or orthodox answers, and these answers have served since then in time-honored fashion down to our own time in the twentieth century.

Another dimension of what happened between the writing of the New Testament and A.D. 451 concerns the character of the changes in the theological discussions. One important change deals with the categories used to describe Jesus. The writers of the Gospels used stories and narratives to identify Jesus. We read about his deeds and his teaching and his interaction with the people and

4. A third classic question posed but unanswered in the New Testament is that of the work of Christ, sometimes called atonement. As John Driver has pointed out so well, the New Testament has a number of images of atonement, but does not resolve the question of how Jesus' life, teaching, death, and resurrection achieve salvation and impact on us. See John Driver, *Understanding the Atonement for the Mission of the Church* (Scottdale/Kitchener: Herald Press, 1986).

5. Space does not permit analysis of these rejected options in this paper. They include such titles as dynamistic and modalistic monarchianism, adoptionism, gnosticism, Sabellianism, docetism, Ebionitism, Arianism, Apollinarianism, Eutychianism, Nestorianism, and so on. See any of the standard histories of doctrine for a discussion of these positions.

the social structures around him. It is these things which-give Jesus his unique identity. They show what it meant for Jesus to be Messiah, how Jesus acted as the Messiah God had sent. These actions contrasted with expectations in the popular mind that the Messiah would lead some kind of revolt against Rome and restore the monarchy.

The narrative character of theological identity appears in another way in several sermons of the book of Acts. These sermons depict the content of the church's proclamation about Jesus in the first weeks after he was no longer with them bodily. The sermons follow a clear outline which says that in the fullness of God's time or as a continuation of the history of God's people, Israel, Jesus came and lived among them, they crucified him, God then raised him from the dead, the speaker has witnessed these things, and on the basis of these events the hearers may receive forgiveness of sins. (See Acts 2:14-39; 3:13-26; 4:10-12; 5:30-32; 10:36-43; 13:17-41.) That outline tells a story, and it is that story which identifies Jesus. When the apostles were asked why they spoke as they did, or in whose name they dared to act as they did, they replied with that story.

As was noted above, by the time we get to Nicea and Chalcedon, Jesus is being defined in entirely different categories. In a phrase, there was a shift from narrative to ontological categories when talking about Jesus. The ontological categories function somewhat like generic categories. Jesus is identified in terms of essential (generic) categories to which he belongs—humanity and deity—rather than in terms of the unique way he was a human being or how he specifically made God's presence known. As an analogy, one might compare narrative versus generic descriptions of Jesus with the way college students could identify me as their professor. The ontological or generic parallel is to discuss the nature or essence of college professors in general—they give lectures, they grade exams and term papers, they have lots of books in their offices, they write essays and books, they advise students, and so on, and then identify me as one who belonged to the essence of that category of people. The narrative parallel describes the activities of a specific professor—he is *the one who* always comes to class two minutes late, who talks about his handball skills, who has a two-year old pile of papers on his desk, who writes on the board a lot, and so on. In this analogy, it is obvious that the narrative description informs us much more about a specific teacher than does the generic description. There seems to be a similar loss of Jesus' particular identity when one moves from the Gospels to Nicea and Chalcedon. The latter say nothing specific about Jesus' deeds or teaching.

The shift from narrative to ontological categories has an additional dimension. Glance again at the definitions of Nicea and Chalcedon cited above. When Jesus' existence on earth is mentioned at all, it is only at birth and death. The plot line goes directly from birth to death, vaulting over his life and teaching. That omission complements the switch from narrative to ontological categories as the foundational way of identifying who Jesus is.

A change in the meaning of the term *Son of God* illustrates another kind of shift which occurred between the time of Jesus' death and the definition of Nicea. Son of God applies to several kinds of figures in the Bible, which include the king of Israel (Ps. 2:7), and Israel as God's chosen people (Exod. 4:22; Jer. 31:9,20). Jesus used the term to identify those who do the will of God (Matt. 5:9,45). Son of God denotes a relationship which links heaven and earth, a relationship between God and someone who inhabits the earthly realm. The title also is used in a special way for Jesus—he is the Son of God in a way that no one else is. Even here, however, the term designates the connection between the heavenly Father and earthly Jesus. Further, Jesus carries out his role as Son in such a way as to incorporate believing men and women, by adoption, into the relationship of sonship to God, a relationship which Jesus has in an inherent and essential and preeminent way. (See, for example, Gal. 4:1-7.) As Son, Jesus is the norm for all who would be God's children. *Son of God* is not therefore the term which best proclaims the deity of Jesus,[6] and one should avoid assuming that the term in

6. The New Testament's highest term for Jesus is *Lord*, a term which carried connotations of deity when the Romans proclaimed, "Caesar is Lord." Christians countered with the profession, "Jesus is Lord."

the New Testament means "offspring of God."[7]

The image and meaning of *Son of God* had changed considerably by the time of the Council of Nicea. Simply put, it no longer designated a relationship between God and the earthly realm but a relationship entirely within the heavenly realm, a relationship within the Godhead itself. When applied to Jesus by theologians of the time, the term did mean something like offspring of God. Since they attributed that meaning to the term, they had to find a way to use it in that manner without either becoming guilty of polytheism or of making Jesus into a lesser or subordinate god. (The language from Nicea and of the Trinity became their solution.) Awareness of this shift in meaning requires us to be careful how we use the term *Son of God*.

There is one final element of theological change which is relevant for the present discussion. Between the New Testament and the time of the definitions of Nicea and Chalcedon, there was a considerable narrowing down of the ways used to describe Jesus' relationship to God and Jesus' lordship of all reality. John 1 uses the Greek concept of Word, Colossians 1 places Jesus over the celestial powers, Hebrews discusses Jesus in terms of sacrificial intermediaries, Philippians 2 uses the image of a new Adam, while Revelation (See esp. Rev. 5–7.) depicts Jesus as the key to the meaning of history.[8] In every case, when the New Testament theologian took the story of Jesus into another cultural setting with a different worldview or cosmology, he used the terminology of the new worldview, but in a way which placed Jesus above it but also confessed him as simultaneously subject to it in human form. The point here is not to discuss these New Testament Christological

---

7. For example, see Oscar Cullmann, *The Christology of the New Testament*, rev. ed. (Philadelphia: Westminster, 1963), pp. 270-305; C. F. D. Moule, *The Origin of Christology* (Cambridge: Cambridge University Press, 1977), pp. 22-31; James D. G. Dunn, *Christology in the Making* (Philadelphia: Westminster, 1980), pp. 12-64.

8. John H. Yoder used these texts and their worldviews as the basis for a discussion of Jesus as the particular reference point for universal truth as a response to the modern world which makes axiomatic the relativity of truth. See Yoder's '"But We Do See Jesus': The Particularity of Incarnation and the Universality of Truth," in *The Priestly Kingdom: Social Ethics as Gospel* (Notre Dame: University of Notre Dame, 1984), pp. 46-62.

images for themselves, but to point out that the Nicene definition has selected out one of them—that of John 1—as the primary one. From the New Testament to Nicea, there has been a narrowing down of the images in which theologians—even the theologians of the Bible— talked about the nature and role of Jesus.

These changes between the New Testament and the definitions of Nicea and Chalcedon continue today to be the subject of a great deal of discussion by theologians and historians of theology. The following isolates two particular ways that these changes pose a significant problem for the way believers' church people should view Christology.

A first and very important point concerns ethics. For Anabaptists, a key dimension of ethics has centered around the term *discipleship*. Discipleship is a shorthand way to say that Jesus—his life and teaching—are normative for the Christian life. In other words, those who would be Christian must live like Christ lived. The definitions of Nicea and Chalcedon are not helpful for discipleship. Stated most baldly, one cannot follow, be a disciple of, a Jesus who is defined only in terms of the generic categories of humanity and deity. It is precisely the elements which fell out of view between the New Testament and Nicea—the life and teaching of Jesus—which are necessary for discipleship. That fact should help us to understand that Nicea-Chalcedon is not a lens through which to read the New Testament, nor can Nicea-Chalcedon alone serve as the norm which tells us whether we have read the New Testament correctly. In fact, when we start with the New Testament, we discover that it applies an important corrective to their definitions.

A further point related to ethics deals with the separation of the death and resurrection of Christ from Christology. Stated another way, since these fourth- and fifth-century definitions do not speak to atonement or the work of Christ, they have separated atonement from Christology. The way in which Jesus died and the purpose for which Jesus died are not a part of the discussion of the nature of Jesus in the Nicene and Chalcedonian formulas. For Mennonites and other peace people, the manner in which Jesus died—nonviolently and nonresistantly—is crucial for people who profess Jesus as normative for their lives.[9]

These theological developments between the New Testament and Nicea-Chalcedon did not take place in a vacuum. The following section of the paper describes the historical context which allowed them to happen.

The impact of Constantinianism

Between the time of the New Testament and the Council of Nicea, the status of the church in relation to the surrounding society underwent a dramatic reversal. While the change actually took place gradually over at least two centuries, the reign of Roman Emperor Constantine is often referred to as a symbol of the shift.[10] When Constantine declared Christianity a legal religion of the empire in A.D. 313, the status of the church was transformed from that of an illegal and sometimes persecuted minority to that of the favored—established—religion of the empire. It changed from an alternative to Roman society to a supporter of Roman society.

For the argument of this paper, two dimensions of the shift are particularly important.[11] One is the change in the

---

9. Other questions about the formulas of Nicea and Chalcedon deal with issues of concern to all Christian traditions. For example, one question concerns language and the meaning of some key concepts. Particularly crucial is the meaning of the term *person*, which is used to designate the three beings of God in the Trinity, with Jesus as the second person. When used in the fourth and fifth centuries, *person* meant something like personage, or the several roles an actor might play in a one-person theater piece. In our era, *person* means much more. The term now means an individual personality and independent will. Those additional meanings give the persons of the Trinity a different connotation than the phrase had in the fourth century. For two good summaries of issues about Nicea and Chalcedon raised by recent scholars and churchmen, see the following: George W. Stroup, "Chalcedon Revisited," *Theology Today* 35.2 (April 1978), pp. 52-64; and Gerald O'Collins, S.J., *What Are They Saying About Jesus?* (Mahwah, N.J.: Paulist Press, 1982).

10. That is, the argument in this paper does not depend on the details of Constantine's life but on the nature of the changes which his regime symbolized. See note 15 for a somewhat more extended example of how Constantine's policy reflected these changes. For the overall story of Constantine, see A. H. M. Jones, *Constantine and the Conversion of Europe* (New York: Macmillan, 1948; reprint, Toronto: University of Toronto, 1978) and Ramsay MacMullen, *Constantine* (Dial Press, 1969; reprint, London: Croom Helm, 1987).

11. This discussion of the implications of the so-called Constantinian shift follows John H. Yoder, "The Constantinian Sources of Western Social Ethics," in *Priestly Kingdom*, pp. 135-47.

institution which bears God's providence in history, namely, the shift from church to civil government and empire as God's agent. That change concerns the identity of the institution which carries and makes visible God's providence in history and in the world. Prior to Constantine, it was the church—the people of God—which represented God's working in history. Since the minority church in a relatively inhospitable world always felt itself in a precarious position and on the verge of extinction, it took faith to say that God was in control of history. The way that the church lived made it very clear, however, that the church existed over against the world or in a state of confrontation with the world.

Parallel to the shift from church to empire as the institutional bearer of God's providence was the shift from Jesus to the emperor as the norm by which to judge the behavior of Christians. Stated in oversimplified fashion, the pre-Constantinian church looked to Jesus the Lord as the norm of faith and practice, and faithfulness to that norm constituted the decisive ethical impulse. Being Christian meant to live the life modeled by Jesus, the head or lord of the church. A person loyal to Rome and to the Roman emperor lived by a different standard than did Christians. Once Christianity became the religion of the empire and it was assumed that the success—survival—of Christianity was linked to the survival of the empire, preservation of the empire became the decisive criterion for ethical behavior. And the emperor or ruler became the norm against which to judge the rightness of a behavior such as killing or truth telling.[12] The operative question became not, What would Jesus do? but, What if the emperor did it? or, What if everyone did it? The clear implication of the question was that if everyone—and most of all the emperor—followed Jesus, it would make the empire vul-

12. It should be emphasized that this development was not caused by Constantine alone, and that the shift is not simply a matter of chronology alone. In fact, the desire to affirm the status quo is already visible in the Old Testament in the tension between prophet and priest or king, so that Constantinianism has always tempted God's people.

nerable to alien invaders.[13] Since the post-Constantinian church now assumed that the empire reflected God's providence, Christians came to believe that it was more important for them to preserve the empire than to live the teachings of Jesus. As a result of the shift from Jesus to the emperor as the standard for ethics, there was a marked change in the ethical standards of the church. Being Christian came to mean adherence to a minimum standard of social behavior. The idea was abandoned that the so-called hard sayings of Jesus applied to all Christians, and the teaching and example of Jesus were no longer assumed to apply to the lives of ordinary Christians.[14]

After the shift symbolized by Constantine, the empire identified itself with the cause of Christianity, and the success (or failure) of the empire corresponded to the success (or failure) of Christianity.[15] The church's status had changed vis-a-vis the empire, and the church could sit comfortably with the social structures around it. The church no longer confronted empire and society; instead, the church supported and was supported—established—by the empire. However, this change in the status of the church also meant that the institution which seemed to make visi-

---

13. For Americans, the modern equivalent of these questions is something on the order of, What about the Russians (or the Libyans or the currently designated national enemy)? As that question is posed today, the questioner assumes that one must abandon the teaching of Jesus in order to defend the United States against the Russians or Libyans or whomever.

14. Two differing institutional objections to the Constinianization of the church were the Donatist movement and the monastic movement. Donatism upheld a higher standard as a separatist movement. From a position within the church, monasticism gave visibility to a higher standard of Christian conduct for those who chose it.

15. Constantine considered the success of his endeavors, particularly successes in battle, as a sign of divine favor, and by his espousal of Christianity he meant to choose the most powerful protector, the true God above all others. Conversely, the assumption about divine support also posed the possibility of failure or punishment if Constantine and the empire failed properly to worship and honor this God. Thus Constantine saw a clear link between the success of his empire and the success of Christianity. His desire to ensure divine favor on his empire by producing a unified church which would placate the god of Christianity motivated Constantine to intervene in such church affairs as the Donatist schism and the Arian controversy. In this assumption that the emperor was responsible for true worship and service of the gods, Constantine was following the already established imperial pattern, while substituting the Christian God for the pagen deities. See analysis and comments throughout Jones, *Constantine and the conversion of Europe* and MacMullen, *Constantine*.

ble God's providence was no longer the church but the empire. Whereas before the church was visible, one needed faith to see God's direction of history; now God's providential guidance of history seemed visible with the success of the Christian empire and it took faith to declare the existence of a committed Christian community within the nominally religious masses of the empire.

It is these shifts in the norm for the definition of Christian behavior and in the institution which reflects God's providence that constitute the context in which to examine the changes in Christology during the first centuries of Christian history. When the church no longer has a sense that every Christian follows Jesus, it is no longer necessary to retain the narratives of Jesus—the specific way in which he was human and revealed the will of God on earth—as part of the discussion of who Jesus was. While those stories were not forgotten by the theologians of the church, they did abandon the idea that the narratives belonged in an essential way to the definition of who he was. It was not necessary to know the specifics of Jesus' life if one was not going to follow Jesus. By the time of the Council of Nicea, the church and her theologians have changed their assumptions about Christology. In contrast to the pre-Constantinian church, they no longer assume that Jesus is normative for ethics, and that outlook is reflected in the emergence of Christological definitions which omit references to the life and teaching of Jesus.

This shift in the social context of Christology took place gradually. It was not the case that the theologians of the time perceived immediately a new ecclesiology and then set out to develop a different statement of Christology to match it. Rather the change in ecclesiology happened gradually, in an evolutionary manner. Eventually there simply came a time when there was no longer an impulse to identify Jesus—define Christology—in a way which could be followed. And the church which did not make Jesus normative—the established church tradition—has accepted that Christology ever since.

Emperor Constantine involved himself personally in the council at Nicea. Constantine himself had called the council to deal with the Christological controversy sparked by Arias, a priest from the North African city of Alexandria, when that controversy threatened to divide Constantine's empire along Greek and Roman cultural lines. He wanted a united church in order to preserve the unity of the empire. In other words, the council was a matter of political expedience as well as a search for theological truth.

In the debates at the council, it was Constantine who proposed and argued for the term "same substance as the Father," which became the operative words of the Nicene formula. All but two participants in the council affirmed the term and rejected the formula proposed by the controversial Arias. The choice of language had a degree of expediency attached to it. In the period after the council, when the supporters of Arias gained the upper hand politically, Constantine threw his support to them and banished Bishop Athanasius, the opponent of Arias. The cycle repeated itself several times, and Athanasius endured banishment a total of five times. When Constantine finally requested baptism on his deathbed, the Arians were in favor, and an Arian baptized Constantine.

These observations concerning Constantine's role in the Council of Nicea do not in themselves necessarily render the traditional Christology false. The Nicene formula is still one kind of answer—a time-honored answer—to a question posed by the New Testament. However, these events do help us to understand the significance of the distance between the New Testament and the time of the council. And they remind us that in analyzing and debating the definitions of Nicea and Chalcedon, we are discussing formulas stated by people gathering at a conference—just as people gathered at Normal, Illinois, in August 1989, to discuss Christology. It is normal (readers may consider that a pun if they wish!) to probe Constantine's choice of words just as certainly as we can ask questions about language used at the Normal gathering.

Although these traditional Christological definitions have shortcomings when viewed from a perspective which assumes the normativeness of Jesus for ethics, they are nonetheless the dominant and received tradition. Since the fifth century, all Christological discussions have dealt with them in some way. The following section provides brief glimpses of some ways Anabaptists have dealt with those formulas.

Sixteenth-century Anabaptism

Sixteenth-century Anabaptists, the historical movement from which Mennonites developed, inherited the definitions of Nicea and Chalcedon, just as did every other group which made up what we call the Protestant Reformation. Not surprisingly, therefore, along with magisterial or state church Protestantism, the Anabaptist theological writings reflect the traditional vocabulary and the traditional outline of Trinitarianism, and the language of Jesus as "truly God and truly man."

At the same time, as the introduction of this essay noted, Anabaptists and Mennonites have frequently found themselves standing over against the other Protestant communions as well as against Catholicism. That social and historical stance has sometimes resulted in a bit of tension between the theological views of Anabaptists and Mennonites and those of the groups which stood over against them. The tension was not always recognized and, in fact, often went unarticulated. Those who did feel it, expressed it in different ways. Nonetheless, out of the maelstrom created by the intersection of Anabaptists with other Christian groups emerged some theological statements which reflected again the pre-Constantinian assumptions about discipleship and the normativeness of Jesus.

In particular, that tension brought some restructuring or changing of emphasis in the received Christology. Anabaptists gave more attention to the Gospels and to the narratives about Jesus than to the theological letters of Paul. They placed more emphasis on ethics and the nature of the redeemed life than in the formula for justification by faith. We note here several examples.

The Christology of Anabaptist Hans Denck (ca. 1500-1527) reflected the tradition of medieval mysticism.[16] His

16. Mystics believed that through prayer and meditation, one could empty oneself and become nothing; and that at the point of becoming nothing, God enters and fills the person. For the time of this period of ecstasy, the person was in *mystical* union with God.

primary focus was on Christ the Word who dwells within every human heart.[17] Except for Anabaptists, the Protestant reformers of the sixteenth century accepted predestination as the necessary foundation for the doctrine of justification by faith. Denck appealed to the indwelling Christ in his refutation of Martin Luther's teaching about predestination. With the Word—Christ—within every heart, Denck reasoned, no one could claim not to have heard the call of God. At the same time, the initiative in the call came from God, and the power to respond to the call came from the Christ within. With this formula, Denck wanted to say that each individual chooses whether or not to come to God, but that the initiative and the power to do so remains nonetheless with the Father. Denck also wanted to say that the one who followed the Word within would lead a changed, righteous life, a life in conformity to that Word. Further, a norm exists, Denck said, against which to measure that new, righteous life. That norm is Jesus of Nazareth. Since Jesus of Nazareth embodied the Word in a way that no one else ever could or did, he stands as the preeminent example of life lived under the aegis of the Word which indwells every heart. Rejection of the use of the sword was one of the most visible ways that the righteous life manifested itself.

In this outlook, Denck referred to Father, Son, and Holy Spirit. One can observe that he had a formal allegiance to and understanding of the triune God. His is not a traditional formulation of Trinitarian thought, however. In fact, Denck's theological emphases were elsewhere. His interest was in refuting predestination in a way which left the salvific initiative with God but preserved the free will of the believer. To analyze Denck's theology only in terms of traditional Trinitarian thought—he has been both rejected as unorthodox and salvaged for traditionalism—is to miss the real import of his outlook.

Over against Denck's stress on the Christ within, Pilgram Marpeck focused on a Jesus external to the believer.

17. See Hans Denck, "Whether God Is the Cause of Evil," in George H. Williams and Angel M. Mergal, eds., *Spiritual and Anabaptist Writers*, Library of Christian Classics, vol. 25 (Philadelphia: Westminster, 1957), pp. 86-111.

For Marpeck, it was this external Jesus who was the means to knowing God the Father and the means to an inward experience of God. At this level, Marpeck shared the beginning point of an external Jesus with Martin Luther rather than with mystical Anabaptist Hans Denck. However, in contrast to Luther, Marpeck assumed the normative nature of earthly Jesus. Jesus was not only the means to knowing God the Father. He was also the norm by which believing persons oriented their conduct, including such issues as the ceremonies of the church and the use of the sword.[18]

Thus, as was the case for Denck, we misunderstand Marpeck's orientation if we read him only in terms of his ability to fit within the theological categories of the traditional theology. On those points, he would appear orthodox and Protestant. In fact, Marpeck had a different orientation, one which does not fit precisely within orthodox Protestantism.

Menno Simons provides yet a third example of why it is misleading to categorize Anabaptists solely on the basis of the traditional terminology. On the one hand, Menno uses a great deal of the traditional vocabulary. He has a Trinitarian outlook, and he takes pains to affirm the humanity and deity of Jesus.[19] On the other hand, Menno's Christology was certainly nonstandard, if not even heretical, when judged by the definition of Chalcedon. Menno followed Melchior Hoffman in developing a "celestial flesh" Christology. Stated in oversimplified fashion, Menno believed that Jesus' flesh was human flesh, but it was a human flesh which he had brought with him from heaven. Thus the heavenly Word became flesh *in* Mary but not *of* Mary; Mary nourished Jesus' flesh, but the flesh came not from Mary but from heaven. Menno used the analogy of a field

---

18. Comments on aspects of Christology are scattered throughout Marpeck's writings. For representative statements, one might see William Klassen and Walter Klaassen, trans. and eds., *The Writings of Pilgram Marpeck*, Classics of the Radical Reformation, vol. 3 (Kitchener/Scottdale: Herald Press, 1978), pp. 75-76, 78-85, 98-100, 212, 233, 274, 314-15, 332, 378-79, 412-14, 434-36, 440, 447, 507-15.

19. For the more helpful sections of Menno's writings, see *The Complete Writings of Menno Simons, c.1496-1561*, trans. Leonard Verduin, ed. John C. Wenger, (Scottdale: Herald Press, 1956), pp. 422-40, 487-98, 763-72, 792-834.

which receives seed from a sower; while the field nourishes and grows the crop, the seeds come from outside and are not of the nature of the field. If one applies the definition of Chalcedon in strict fashion, Menno's view is unacceptable. Flesh which came from heaven is simply not genuine *human* flesh.

Menno's Christology reflected one kind of medieval misunderstanding about human reproduction, namely that at conception, the male implanted a complete human being into the womb of the female, where it grew until ready for birth. With that model in mind, Menno believed that Jesus must have begun from the Word which entered Mary and became flesh. Menno's intention was good. He wanted to define Christology in such a way as to ensure the sinlessness of Jesus while also preserving the unity of Jesus' person.[20] For Menno, emphasis on the flesh of Jesus affirmed his humanity, while the heavenly origin of the Word affirmed Jesus' deity while also preserving the unity of Jesus' person. Menno wanted to defend the sinlessness of Jesus because he believed that the church founded by Jesus was a pure church and an extension of Jesus' work on earth. Menno also describes the process of change and conversion in the life of the sinner so that he or she is transformed in an incomplete way into the flesh of Christ, a transformation which will find its fulfillment at the return of Jesus. Thus while he got there by a quite different route than did Denck and Marpeck, Menno too is oriented by what can be called discipleship, the idea that the earthly life of Jesus constitutes an example and a norm for the life of Christian believers.

We miss entirely the theological significance of these three Anabaptists if we interpret them only in terms of their use of the language of Trinity and of Jesus as human and divine. At that level, these three appear variously either as slightly suspicious versions of Protestant orthodoxy or merely less significant versions of Protestantism.

20. Traditional Catholic thought tried to solve this problem through the doctrine of the immaculate conception of Mary. To give Jesus a sinless mother from whom he could then inherit sinless flesh, Catholic thought posited a miraculous, immaculate conception of Mary—one in which the Holy Spirit prevented the transmission of original sin through the sex act.

However, when we look at them from a stance of awareness of the implications of the Constantinian synthesis (its assumption that Jesus' life and teaching are not normative, and that atonement is separated from Christology), then we see these Anabaptist statements as attempts to recover the theological framework which the church abandoned in the course of the second, third, and fourth centuries of the church.

The normativeness of Jesus

If today Mennonites and believers' church people are asking questions and discussing the traditional definitions of Christology, then we are part of a long tradition of persons engaging in that task. Although it has not always been articulated as an ecclesiological problem, Anabaptist and Mennonite and believers' church formulations on Christology have sometimes reflected the tension of trying to hold together the understanding of an alternative church with a received Christology developed by the established church. This is the tension between an assumption that being Christian means discipleship (following Jesus) and an established church tradition which does not make Jesus' life normative for the Christian life. Today, in particular because of the growing realization by all churches of the demise of Christendom, that tension between an alternative or believers' church ecclesiology and an established church Christology is becoming more explicit, not only for Mennonites but for many theological traditions.

Mennonites have expressed and responded to the tension in a variety of ways. Their answers have enabled observers to interpret Anabaptists and Mennonites as both orthodox (they used the traditional language of Nicea, the Cappadocians, and Chalcedon) and original or radical or unorthodox (they revised or altered or added to the traditional language). Some modern Mennonite theologians want to make the fourth- and fifth-century language the foundation of modern Mennonite systematic theology. And precedents do exist for that procedure. However, offering an alternative to that ancient language is not so much a departure from orthodoxy as it is a statement that Christology for the believers' church should correspond to believers' church assumptions and ecclesiology rather than to established church presuppositions.

One can also pose the question of the final truth of Nicea-Chalcedon in terms of a view of where God's people are visible in history. Clearly there was an unfolding of and development of doctrine between the writing of the New Testament and the Council of Chalcedon in the middle of the fifth century. But was the path taken inevitable, was that theology inevitably and inherently true, and was it lacking any impact of the church's changed status from the persecuted to the supporter of Roman civilization? Must we accept unreservedly the doctrine which unfolded within the history of a church becoming an established church? This chapter has answered in the negative. I argued that the Christological formulations traditionally accepted as orthodox reflect the understandings of the Constantinian church, the church which did not make Jesus' life and teaching normative for the Christian life. Adherents of the believers' churches may legitimately look for historical precedents of Christology which accept the normative nature of Jesus' life, and they ought not to shy away from continuing to articulate that kind of Christology today.[21] Stating the question most boldly, Is there true theology which does not, or need not, pass through the Constantinian church? I believe there is.

Such a conclusion is in no way to doubt biblical truth. The Bible remains our foundation and guide. The conclusion does express a choice about the tradition through whose eyes we will read the Bible with most confidence, that of the Constantinian church or of the believers' church.

May God guide our continuing deliberations about Christology. In discussing it, we are part of a long tradition. In asking questions and critiquing the received definitions, we are also part of a long tradition. May respect for the received definitions not blind us to the importance

21. C. Norman Kraus, *Jesus Christ Our Lord: Christianity from a Disciple's Perspective* (Scottdale/Kitchener: Herald Press, 1987) is one recent effort to do Christology in this fashion.

of the normativensss of Jesus and to the call to give expression to his normative life through a church which poses an alternative to the world.

Die warhayt ist untödtlich.

**I thank Ted Grimsrud, Burton Yost, and Alain Epp, each of whom read drafts of this manuscript and made suggestions which were incorporated into the final edition.

Still something essential in the creeds

Response to "Christology in Historical Perspective"

Thomas Finger

Jesus has always been at the center of Mennonite faith. Mennonites have almost always studied and pondered his *work*—his teachings, his example, his cross—and emphasized the importance of following these. In many times and places, however, we have not reflected as explicitly on the question of Jesus' *person*—who he really was and is. Sometimes, when Mennonites formed tight-knit communities relatively isolated from the larger world, there was little felt need to articulate, either for ourselves or others, our implicit convictions on this theme. We were little involved in mission, and the question of identity, of what it meant to be Mennonite, could be largely resolved by ethical and cultural criteria.

J. Denny Weaver, however, has persuasively argued that Mennonite identity (and surely mission too) can no longer be determined solely by these means. As we live among groups and trends which were once quite foreign, and as people from these worlds join us, the question of who we are, or should be, has grown increasingly problematic. It is becoming clearer, though, that we are essentially a religious group. Our lives are rooted in relationship with God. Consequently, Weaver argues, the emerging expression of our identity must be partly *theological*: must involve explicit articulation of those implicit beliefs that have always guided us.[1]

This means, in reference to Jesus, that we must speak of more than his teaching, example, or even his cross. For Mennonites have always believed that Jesus brings us into eternal relationship with God. And while Jesus' teaching, example, and cross are essential means to this, we must be more explicit about how he is related to (and mediates this communion with) God. In other words, we must ponder not only Jesus' work, but also his person.

The desire for theological articulation is emerging in many ways. The General Conference and the Mennonite Church are developing a joint confession of faith. Mennonite World Conference is launching a global faith and life study pointing towards some kind of statement at Winnipeg in 1990.[2] And whereas past assemblies of the Mennonite Church and General Conference have generated few seminars on theological themes, the 1989 joint assembly at Normal attracted 800 persons—including Mennonite Brethren and Brethren in Christ—to a two-day Study Conference on Christology. Denny Weaver's essay, "Christology in Historical Perspective," on which I will now comment, was a preparatory reading for this gathering.

When Christians of almost any denomination, including Mennonites, discuss who Jesus is, a certain phrase will nearly always emerge. People who have thought about the matter at all will usually have heard somewhere that Jesus is fully God and fully human. For some this affirmation is problematic. They are sure that Jesus was fully human; but if so, how could he actually *be* God? Others, however, find confession of Jesus' full deity essential to their faith, even if that makes it confusing about how he could be truly human.

Many Christians, of course, know nothing about the origins of this phrase. Weaver usefully shows how it comes chiefly from the Nicene Creed (325 A.D.) and the Chalcedonian Creed (451 A.D.). And by discussing the philosophical

---

1. J. Denny Weaver, "Mennonites: Theology, Peace and Identity," *Conrad Grebel Review*, Vol. 6, No. 2 (Spring, 1988), pp. 119-145.

2. See the study book for this process, *Witnessing to Christ in Today's World*, by Helmut Harder, published 1989 by Evangel Press, Faith and Life Press, Kindred Press, and Mennonite Publishing House for the Mennonite World Conference.

and sociopolitical contexts in which these creeds were for-
mulated, Weaver highlights some drawbacks they can have
for Mennonite Christological reflection.

Weaver argues, first, that these creeds are *incomplete*.
They omit affirmations that Mennonites want to make
about Jesus. Moreover, these omissions, appreciated in
light of the creeds' sociopolitical context, concern matters of
special significance for us. Weaver seems to argue further,
however, that these creeds are relatively *inconsequential*
for current Mennonite reflection. While the creeds deserve
respect as important historical formulations, their chief
affirmations need have little impact upon Christology
today. (Someone, extending some of Weaver's arguments,
might also claim that the creeds are *incorrect*. I do not see
Weaver taking this step.)

When Weaver argues that the creeds are incomplete, I
find him generally convincing. But insofar as he claims
that they are largely inconsequential, I have serious reservations. I will divide my responses under these two head-
ings.

The creeds are incomplete

Denny Weaver rightly complains that neither the Nicene
nor the Chalcedonian Creeds really deal with Jesus' life
and teachings. They move directly from his birth to his
death. In this and other ways they omit reference to the
life of discipleship.[3] Weaver also claims that these creeds
fail to deal with atonement, with the "way in which Jesus
died and the purpose for which Jesus died...." (p. 93). I find
this latter point a bit overstated. Both creeds say that
Jesus came "for our salvation," and, as Weaver notes, a

---

3. Actually, the Nicene Creed of 325 A.D., as quoted by Weaver, simply says
that the Son "became man, suffered, and rose...." It is possible that the suffering
was understood to relate to Jesus' whole life. The form of the Nicene Creed now
accepted by churches, however, is the expanded form promulgated by the Council of
Constantinople in 381 (and technically called the Nicene-Constantinopolitan Creed).
Instead of simply saying "suffered," this creed reads, "was crucified for us under
Pontius Pilate, suffered, was buried and rose...." The later creed also expands on the
role of the Holy Spirit, and adds belief in the church, baptism, and forgiveness of
sins. Some would argue that these additions point in some measure to the Christian
life.

main purpose of the Nicene Creed was "to secure the divine origin of salvation" (p. 86).

Nonetheless, Weaver's major criticism stands. Since the creeds lay great emphasis on what they assert—they threaten dissenters with excommunication—and since they say little or nothing about discipleship and salvation, they can create the impression that being Christian is mostly a matter of verbal affirmation, and that the way one lives is largely irrelevant.

Weaver also complains that the creeds overlook the rich multiplicity of images and concepts with which the Bible describes Jesus. Instead, "the Nicene definition has selected out one of them—that of John 1—as the primary one" (p.93). I am not sure what this sentence means. The Nicene Creed uses the biblical titles Lord, Son, only-begotten, begotten, light, truth, and "through whom all things were made." While all these appear in John 1, only the third and fourth are chiefly Johannine. The rest occur in many other places. And the foremost title of John 1, "Word," does not appear in the creed.

Nevertheless, Weaver's main point is again correct. The discussions leading to Nicea and Chalcedon usually focused on a few titles—Word, Son, only-begotten—while others, especially those relevant for discipleship, fell into the background. These discussions also centered on a few themes, on those associated with Jesus' deity and humanity. Yet other paradoxes of Jesus' person might have claimed equal attention. What, for instance, did it mean that the Lord of all had lived among us as a servant? That the true king had favored the poor? That the author of life had suffered an ignominious, accursed death? Such central Christological issues, which carry implications for sociopolitical life, tended to fade from view.

Given the selectivity that governed the creeds' formation, Weaver rightly insists that we misappreciate Anabaptist Christologies if we simply note where they conform or diverge from the former, and treat the rest as variations on a common theme. Denck, Marpeck and Menno were reopening issues that had been largely lost. Similarly, current Mennonite reflection should approach Jesus from various angles. If we ponder the Scriptures' variety and the insights of our own tradition, we will be enriched, and have much to offer other denominations.

Are the creeds inconsequential?

A theological affirmation could be incomplete but still be important. While not saying everything, it could still say something essential. Denny Weaver, however, seems to argue, or at least strongly imply, that the Nicene and Chalcedonian Creeds are not only incomplete, but also relatively inconsequential for contemporary Mennonite reflection. He concludes by affirming that there is a "true theology which does not, or need not, pass through the Constantinian church" (p. 104).

Weaver apparently arrives at this conclusion by two major routes. First, he argues that the New Testament and the creeds speak of Jesus "in entirely different categories" (p. 90). The speech of the former is narrative; it identifies Jesus and his significance by telling of his acts. The language of the latter is ontological; it identifies Jesus in terms of his essence, or being. However, I think that Weaver overdraws this distinction in three ways.

First, the Nicene Creed, at least, preserves the narrative framework of earlier creeds, such as the Apostles' Creed. It tells of the Son who came, suffered, died, rose, ascended and will come again. It contains only one technical term from Greek philosophy: *homoousion* ("of the same substance"). To be sure, this narrative framework nearly vanishes and the ontological terms increase in the Chalcedonian Creed.

Second, and far more important, when Weaver claims that New Testament language is narrative, he refers only to the Synoptic Gospels and Acts. He fails to acknowledge that other writings speak of Jesus in ontological terms. Hebrews, among other things, asserts that he "reflects the glory of God and bears the very stamp of his nature, upholding the universe by the word of his power" (1:3). Such phrases speak not only of how Jesus acts, but of who he most fundamentally is. While similar texts (e.g., John 1:1-19, Phil. 2:5-11, Col. 1:15-20) may be relatively few, their position and significance within the respective books

110

show that they are hardly inconsequential.

Third, Weaver overstates the difference between narrative and ontological language. Narratives about a person raise the question of *identity*, of who this person really is; and when that individual continually acts in God's name, this surely raises the question of that person's being. (Cf. Matt. 16:13-17.) Further, to affirm that a particular person is *divine* is quite different from merely including one in a broad generic classification (such as professor in Weaver's example). It is to make a highly unique and astounding claim about that individual's true identity.

When Weaver calls biblical and creedal language "entirely different categories," I wonder whether he assumes that if one affirms the creeds, one must accept the technical meaning that certain terms (like *homoousion*) apparently had, along with the entire philosophical background from which they came.[4] Careful study, however, shows that ancient theologians understood such terms in various ways, often regarding them as shorthand for more complex biblical notions.

Consequently, affirming that Jesus is "of the same substance" as the Father need not involve accepting any ancient definition of substance or deity. One need only affirm that whatever God is, Jesus is fully that—leaving more precise understandings of deity to be filled in by biblical content. The creeds, that is, affirm chiefly *that* Jesus is divine and human, not *how* he can be both, nor precisely *what* these terms might mean. They provide parameters within which contemporary Christology can work, not detailed definitions which it must accept.

Denny Weaver's second major reason for regarding the creeds as somewhat inconsequential flows from his concentration on their political context. To be sure, Constantine and his successors had much to do with the creeds' incompleteness—their omission of discipleship and its sociopolitical implications—and with the impression that being Christian consisted chiefly in affirming creeds' contents. Weaver explains all this well.

---

4. Norman Kraus' criticisms of the creeds may rest largely on this assumption. See *Jesus Christ our Lord* (Scottdale: Herald, 1987), esp. pp. 47-48, 68, 97-98, 113.

Nevertheless, given our deep Mennonite disapproval of Constantinianism, and given a widespread tendency to assume that the meanings of statements are largely products of their sociopolitical contexts, Weaver's focus on this background can lead one to dismiss the creeds too easily. For Weaver overlooks other contexts essential to their formation.

Although Constantine presided over the sessions at Nicea, these occurred only twelve years after he became the first emperor to favor the church. The ecclesiastical and theological issues discussed there, however, had been developing for over 150 years. Among the theologians contributing to their formation were Justin Martyr (100?-?164) and Origen (186?-?232), both executed for their faith. The foremost architect of the developing Christological conceptuality was probably Tertullian (150?-?230), whose rigorous ethical standards and pneumatic leanings remind one of the Anabaptists.

Of course, the social contexts of these thinkers no more render their theologies correct than does Constantine's influence make the Nicene decisions false. But they do show that it is oversimplified to say that the creeds "reflect the understandings of the Constantinian church" (p. 104). For they also reflect the culmination of discussions pursued and conceptuality developed in the church of the radicals and the martyrs.

Our theological identity

Perhaps Denny Weaver and I agree more than it seems. Perhaps he, like me, merely wishes to emphasize the creeds' incompleteness, their potentially disastrous practical consequences, and the importance of considering other Christological issues.[5] But even should the term "relatively inconsequential" understate his estimate of the creeds' continuing importance, I find it crucial to raise this issue;

5. I have argued that the problems with the Nicene Creed lie not in what it *does* say, but in what it *does not* say, and in the *way* it has been *used*. ("The Way to Nicea: Reflections from a Mennonite Perspective," *Conrad Grebel Review*, Vol. 3, No. 3 [Fall, 1985], pp. 231- 249.) For my own constructive view on the person of Jesus Christ, see my *Christian Theology: An Eschatological Approach*, Vol. II (Scottdale: Herald, 1989), pp. 379-479.

first, because I find no clear affirmation of the creeds' substantive significance in his essay, and second, because this theme is vital for continuing discussion.

The authors writing for the Normal study conference seem divided on this matter. John Toews, sharing Weaver's apparent orientation, asserts that the creeds merely "answered the specific and narrow Christological questions of their time, e.g., was Jesus both human and divine?" (p. 35). In contrast, Harry Huebner, structures his essay around "the moral implications of the Chalcedonian affirmation" (p. 57). And George Brunk III insists that the Chalcedonian Creed could "be abandoned only on overwhelming evidence and after the clear construction of something better" (p. 12, n. 12).

Because of our emphasis on discipleship, because the creeds appear to raise complex metaphysical issues, and because state-supported religion has enforced the creeds, most Mennonites are unfamiliar with them. At this stage of working towards theological identity, it is natural to ask what significance they might have. Still, I strongly doubt that most Mennonites would regard the *major affirmations* of the creeds as "specific and narrow" concerns of a long-gone era.

In a culture where the Jesus we follow often appears as an ethereal figure, is it irrelevant to stress that he was as fully human as we? In times of struggle, is the question of whether he faced the same problems as we do, and on the same terms, inconsequential? And is the issue of whether Jesus was simply a prophet or representative of God, or actually God's own self, unimportant? For if he was fully divine, then the love, the suffering, the death, and the resurrection joy of Jesus were God's very own personal love, suffering, death, and joy. Then God personally experienced those events essential to our human existence and our salvation. But if Jesus was less than fully divine, then God was less directly involved in them.

If we regard the creeds as *inconsequential*, we can come to regard their fundamental concerns as inconsequential too. And then it will matter little whether or not their central affirmations are *incorrect*. I strongly suspect, however, that most Mennonites regard these affirmations as of great consequence and as correct, even though the creedal language is unfamiliar. Accordingly, while we should indeed pursue a variety of Christological issues, neglect of the traditional ones will only confuse our search for theological identity. And in a world where many are asking about our view of Jesus, vagueness as to whether he was merely a human teacher and example, or something more, will hardly help.

Looking for guidelines in the Anabaptist tradition

Response to "Still Something Essential in the Creeds"

J. Denny Weaver

As a whole, I acknowledge and accept the instances of over-simplification or overstatement which Finger pointed out. Finger's nuanced revisions are in order. Although I would like to discuss some of those revisions further, I take the limited space available here to deal more with Finger's response as a whole.

I thank Finger for affirming another of my recent articles in which I argued that theology must be part of modern Mennonite identity, that we must make explicit the previously implicit beliefs which have guided us. My current paper on Christology grows out of that mission to make explicit how our longstanding Anabaptist-Mennonite assumptions—about discipleship, the normativity of Jesus for ethics, the social and communal nature of salvation, the church as a fellowship of believers—can shape the way we talk about issues such as Christology which are on the theological agenda of every tradition.

It could go without saying that I appreciate Finger's agreement with and affirmation of my positions as a whole. Those points of agreement about the classic creeds include, specifically, the incompleteness of the creeds, the impression that being Christian is more a matter of verbal affirmation than of the way one lives, the narrowing down of the biblical images used, the fact that Anabaptist Christologies should not be interpreted solely in terms of conformity or divergence from the classic stance, and the fact that Constantine and his successors had much to do with the incompleteness of the creeds. I want to make explicit one more dimension of agreement which is assumed in both my essay and Finger's response. We both acknowledge, although perhaps not quite to the same extent, that the language of the creeds is not quite the same as the language of the Bible. That is, while the creeds deal with biblical material and provide answers to questions of interpretation posed by the biblical materials, the terminology of the creeds is not always biblical language.

If we agree on the fact that the words of the creeds are not necessarily biblical words, then the discussion is about the guidelines and principles we use to measure whether we have read and interpreted the Bible correctly. As I indicated in my essay, it is at least in part a matter of the historical tradition which we identify as the bearer of God's providence. At that point, it would appear that Finger is a bit more willing than I to affirm that God's providence passes necessarily through the Constantinian church.

There is something paradoxical about Finger's defense of the Nicene- Chalcedonian language or creeds. The higher the status which one wants to accord the creeds as purveyors of truth, the more problematic they become for the Anabaptist-Mennonite and believers' church emphasis on discipleship. That is, the higher the status given to Nicea-Chalcedon as the norm for biblical interpretation, the more serious becomes the fact that they leap over the life and teaching of Jesus and separate Christology from ethics. Thus, in order to save them for the discipleship tradition, it is paradoxically necessary simultaneously to claim less for their status as truth claims by acknowledging their incompleteness and their cultural-relatedness. To claim more, one also claims less. Finger and I are both aware of and working within that paradoxical situation (although, of course, I realize that Finger did not state the paradox in that way). In discussing the proper point to occupy on that paradoxical continuum of acceptance, Finger used the word "inconsequential" to describe my attitude toward the creeds. While he gave no parallel label to his own position, it might describe the classic creeds as "relevant" or even "necessary."

It would appear in Finger's response that he went quite far in recognizing the incompleteness and cultural-relatedness of the creeds. He suggested, for example, that one can accept the creed without accepting the entire philosophical background of terms such as *homoousion*, and that, in fact, the ancient theologians used it as "shorthand for more complex biblical notions." Thus for a modern person to affirm Jesus as "of the same substance" as the Father "need not involve accepting *any* [emphasis mine] ancient definition of substance or deity. One need only affirm that whatever God is, Jesus is fully that—leaving more precise understandings of deity to be filled in by biblical content." I agree with and accept Finger's comment. At the same time, it is also a statement that Finger is willing, as the case may be, to keep the shell and change the kernel, to give new definitions in order to claim to keep the original terms.[1] Whether Finger's statement would make the creed inconsequential or relevant or necessary, I would submit, is more a matter of semantics than of substance. We are, it seems, quite close to the proverbial argument about whether a glass is half full or half empty.

I think that Finger and I have come quite close together while starting from different vantage points. In both his personal background as well as in his academic theological position, Finger begins by wanting to affirm as much as possible of the traditional Christological language while his awareness of the sociopolitical contexts of the first five centuries and his knowledge of the more recent development of the free church, believers' church tradition, the roots of whose modern version are traceable to sixteenth century Anabaptism, both compel and enable him to develop a nuanced stance vis-a-vis the creedal tradition. For Finger, the operative question might be how to modify what we say about the classic creeds enough to be able to accept them

1. For a somewhat different attempt to save the classic creeds by claiming less for them, see Ben C. Ollenburger, "Christology and Creeds," *AMBS Bulletin* 52.3 (May 1989), 2-3.

117

on believers' church principles. In both my personal background as well as academic theological position, I begin with the intent to develop a theology which both complements and reflects the unique ecclesiological stance of the believers' church tradition. My operative question might be how to construct a Christology that depends on the believers' church tradition, which claims that Jesus is normative for ethics, which affirms that ethics is inseparable from Christology, which affirms that Jesus is both Savior and Lord.

My position feels like a rejection of orthodoxy only when one does not have a firm sense of believers' church emphases. Identifying truth with believers' church emphases is a statement about the providential leading of God in history. It is a statement that the will of God and the norm of truth are not inseparably linked to the majority church. What is—the establishment of the church symbolized by Constantine—is not synchronous with God's will or God's providence. The stronger sense one has that God's people and the will of God do not necessarily follow the established church symbolized by Constantine, the more easily can one accept the idea of developing Christology in categories rooted in believers' church emphases. It is because I have such a high sense of God's revelation in Christ that I am reluctant to make the foundation or guidelines of Christology those statements which we recognize as only a partial statement and which are anchored in an ecclesiological line which neglects things I consider part of God's revelation in Christ.

In this kind of theological discussion, Mennonites—in fact, the entire believers' church tradition—are charting a new course. The first conference which began the task of defining a believers' church ecclesiological tradition took place only in 1967.[2] Only one conference in this ongoing series had the agenda of applying that ecclesiological

---

2. June 1967, at Southern Baptist Theological Seminary, Louisville, Kentucky. The papers from that conference were published in James Leo Garrett, Jr., ed., *The Concept of the Believers' Church* (Scottdale, Pa.: Herald Press, 1968).

stance to a theological question,[3] and as John Toews pointed out in his paper for our gathering in Normal, Illinois,
none of the papers from that conference dealt specifically
with the ecclesiological dimensions of Christology. As Mennonites, we have begun formal discussions on Christology
only in the 1980s. We do not yet have a fully articulated
and established tradition in systematic theology which sets
out the guidelines on what a specifically believers' church
Christology should look like. That discussion is precisely
what the current debate is about. In such a new theological game, it is to be expected that there be some disagree-
ments, some oversimplifications, and some new and helpful
directions charted.

My prayer is that we are not so concerned to find God's
providence with the established church tradition that we
miss this opportunity to develop a theology genuinely worthy of our believers' church tradition.

Die warhayt ist untödtlich.

3. The believers' church conference on Christology which met at Bluffton (Ohio)
College in October 1980. For a summary of the presentations from that conference,
see J. Denny Weaver, "A Believers' Church Christology," *Mennonite Quarterly
Review*, 57.2 (April 1983): 112-31.

Contemporary Anabaptist perspectives

Findings Committee Report/Study Conference on Christology

The purpose of the conference was "to enter into serious dialogue concerning our understanding of the person, the work, and the ethical and missiological significance of Jesus Christ in the life and ministry of our people, to clarify our faith positions, to identify areas of commonality and difference, and to promote better mutual understanding and greater unity among our groups as we together witness that *Jesus Christ is Lord.*"

The impetus for the consultation came from the Council of Moderators and Secretaries (of several Mennonite and Brethren in Christ conferences in North America). They planned the consultation as *one step* in following up on the call from the 1984 Strasbourg Missions Consultation (in conjunction with the Mennonite World Conference) to Mennonite groups around the world to give careful attention to their understanding of Jesus Christ (Christology) and the significance of Christology for Christian mission.

The general purpose became more focused and thus more limited in the actual planning and implementation of the conference program. The major presentations and much of the discussion focused on the relation between the doctrine of Jesus Christ (Christology) and the exclusiveness of Jesus Christ in relation to Christian mission, the relation between Christology and the doctrine of the church (ecclesiology), and the relation between Christology and Christian discipleship (ethics). Neither the presentations nor the program nor the amount of time available for discussion therefore could cover the entire range of Christology as the doctrine of the person and work of Jesus Christ.

Four stimulating, provocative, and relevant papers were presented (or included in the preparatory study books) by George R. Brunk III, John E. Toews, Harry Huebner, and J. Denny Weaver. Intense interest was demonstrated by thorough preparation, high attendance, and vigorous discussion. The major theses of the three presentations were both affirmed and challenged. *Discussion groups* grappled primarily with the topics of the three major presentations: the relationship of Christology to the doctrine of the church, to the theology of mission, and to Christian discipleship. Because the Weaver paper was not presented in plenary session, it did not receive extensive attention in the discussion groups. *Focus groups* on particular topics provided opportunities to enlarge the range of discussion somewhat beyond the major presentations.

The consultation was unusual with respect to the scope of its participants. Rather than being limited either to scholars or to ministers or to other interested persons, it included the lively participation of ministers, scholars, and other interested church members from both Canada and the United States. This inclusiveness brought with it the usual challenges of diverse agenda and vocabularies. It also provided a rare opportunity for direct conversation on matters of common—and sometimes differing—concern between representatives of these groups. This kind of conversation may well have been one of the major values of the consultation. The most serious handicap to this conversation's being even more fruitful for the life and teaching of t he church was doubtless the limited amount of time (a little more than one full day) available to work through the challenges of diverse agenda and vocabulary.

This findings report primarily summarizes reports from the twenty-four discussion groups and, in a more limited fashion, from the fourteen focus groups. (See the list of focus groups in the Foreword.) The report generally does

not include matters which were raised in only one group.
The report makes some attempt to assess the relative fre-
quency with which specific issues and questions surfaced
in the groups.

The outline of the report follows the themes of the
three major presentations: Christology and mission, Christology and church, and Christology and ethics (next three
sections). Discussions in the focus groups are treated sepa-
rately (fourth section). The findings committee developed
the synopsis (final section) on the basis of what it heard
from the conference as a whole.

A first draft of this findings report was made available
to participants during the last plenary session of the consultation. Participants made several suggestions for clarifying and modifying the first draft. *This formulation of the
findings report is the findings committee's revised version
based on the initial draft and on the suggested modifica-
tions which appeared to represent the broad support of the
participants during the last plenary discussion.*

Jesus Christ and Christian mission

Brunk's thesis on the exclusiveness of Jesus Christ found
relatively broad agreement and affirmation in the discussion groups (at least 14 groups).

This broad agreement was however qualified in several
ways. Participants in four groups wished to emphasize the
inclusiveness of Jesus. For some, this meant that Jesus
Christ offers salvation to those who have been or are frequently excluded on the basis of obedience to the law, eth-
nic origins, class, and the like. For some, this meant that
salvation through Jesus Christ might include some who
may not have made an explicit faith commitment to him.

Several groups were unsure both about how Brunk
defines exclusiveness and about how the term would best
be understood. Five groups not only raised questions about
the definition of exclusiveness, but disagreed with what
they took to be Brunk's understanding, which appears to
empty the term of its normal meaning and to make Jesus
Christ less exclusive than traditionally assumed.

Many participants strongly affirmed the presentation's

emphasis on the need to maintain and develop irenic mission strategies and non-judgmental attitudes toward non-Christians (11 groups). However opinions about what constitutes the primary Mennonite problem appeared evenly divided: some feel it's a loss of Christological nerve (perhaps more in some Anglo segments of Mennonite groups than among Hispanic and other minority groups); some consider it to be triumphalism (2 groups each). Most agreed with the presentation that claims about the exclusiveness of Jesus Christ should be differentiated from making such claims for the church (or for our enculturated forms of church).

Two major questions on which further clarification would be desirable were raised in several ways. Brunk appears to differentiate between Jesus Christ and the Christian church more than Toews. Ten groups perceived a tension between Toews' and Brunk's presentations in this regard. A number of groups called for clarifying salvation and related concepts. Several groups (4 or 5) wondered whether the apparent revisions in understandings of exclusiveness and salvation (Are there different levels or degrees?) suggested or implied by the paper might in fact weaken missionary motivation. Similar questions were raised about the concepts of revelation and truth.

Jesus Christ and the Christian church

Toews' emphasis upon community as a corrective to North American individualism found broad support (10 groups). This support extended to agreement in five additional groups for the corporate dimensions of salvation outlined in his presentation. Three groups agreed with the close link between Jesus and the church. Simultaneously, many participants voiced strong reservations or disagreement about the degree to which Toews connected Christ and salvation with the church. Several found the assertion that there is no salvation outside the church too strong (6 groups). Others felt that the linkage between Jesus and the church had been overemphasized at the expense of the individual's relation to Jesus Christ (also 6 groups). A number of participants found the emphasis upon binding and loosing, taken together with the focus on the church, too reminiscent of traditional Roman Catholicism (4 groups).

The designation of Jesus as convener of the church elicited agreement, disagreement, and further questions. Participants in seven groups affirmed the concept; those in three groups expressed strong doubts about its usefulness; others asked whether it is synonymous with head (4 groups). A few thought Jesus was more the initiator than the convener of the church.

The methodological approach found both affirmative and critical responses among the discussion groups. Two agreed with the approach which begins with Jesus according to the Synoptic Gospels, moves on to the Epistles, and considers the classical Christian creeds largely irrelevant. An equal number questioned the adequacy of this approach.

Toews' thesis on the close connection between Christology and ecclesiology precipitated a series of questions needing further clarification for many participants. What is salvation and is it to be found primarily in Christ or primarily in the church (10 groups)? What is the relationship between the church and the kingdom of God (5 groups)? What are the practical and theological implications of Toews' thesis (3 groups)? Several groups wondered about the role of the Holy Spirit in relation to the church.

Jesus Christ and Christian ethics

Like Toews' concern for the significance of community, Huebner's understanding of the church as a community of moral discernment found significant affirmation (5 groups). And as with the Toews and Brunk presentations, the responses to the central emphases of Huebner's presentation included both widespread agreement and significant disagreement. Participants in nine groups agreed that Jesus is normative for Christian ethics and those in seven groups that the cross is the paradigm for an ethics of character and virtue. Nevertheless a significant number believed that Huebner overemphasized the ethical relevance of the cross at the expense of the resurrection (7 groups). The same number missed any attention to the transforming energy of God's salvation which enables Christian faithfulness. Almost as many observed that nothing was said about the Holy Spirit's role in relation to Christ and Christian obedience and considered this a serious lack.

Several participants explicitly disagreed with Huebner's focus on the cross as the central model for ethical reflection and considered the cross an inadequate basis for Christian ethics (6 groups). This disagreement was doubtlessly related to the perceived exclusion of the resurrection and the Holy Spirit in developing a basis for discipleship. Several groups also did not understand the reference to worship as "the most profound moral act" or felt that the dimensions of worship and spirituality were unfortunately omitted.

The major questions for further clarification corresponded to the points where participants registered both agreement and disagreement with the presentation. At least five groups wanted further clarification of what is meant by the cross. Others requested an explanation of the cross both as the means of atonement and as the central model for Christian ethics. Several again asked about the role of the Holy Spirit in relation to discipleship.

Focus group discussions

Another important aspect of the conference was the input and discussions in the focus groups. We express appreciation to the leaders for the way their work contributed to a more detailed discussion of many questions which had surfaced in the plenary presentations and in the discussion groups.

As nearly as the findings committee could ascertain, several themes were raised in the focus groups that did not appear in the discussion groups. These included: Christ as Sophia (Wisdom) and Creator, Christ as Liberator, personal experience of Christ, and the implications of the maleness of Jesus from a feminist perspective. Other themes such as the importance of a trinitarian Christology, questions about the classical Christian creeds for Christology in an

Anabaptist perspective, Christ as the self-revelation of God, and doctrines of the atonement were addressed in greater depth than had been possible in the discussion groups.

Synopsis of findings

The following observations arise out of the papers presented, the plenary sessions, and the group discussions.

1. The centrality and significance of Jesus Christ for our understandings and practice of mission, church, and discipleship were broadly reaffirmed. The consultation also confirmed the timeliness and the importance of focusing careful study, corporate worship, and serious conversation on the doctrine of Jesus Christ (Christology) and its implications for several aspects of the church's faith and life.

2. The work and missiological significance of Christ received more attention than his person with the result that we may have learned more about church, missions, and ethics than about Christology. Participants expressed keen appreciation for the opportunity to consider these topics in their relation to Christology. Simultaneously, there was a rather broadly based sense that it would also be equally worthwhile for Mennonite and Brethren in Christ groups to give further explicit attention to Christology in the narrower sense.

3. The close relationship of Christ to the church as a discerning and discipling community was presented and strongly affirmed as both biblical and Anabaptist (Toews, Huebner). However there is a keen sense that the ideal church is not the actual church and that God's work is not confined to the actual church (Brunk). This contrast raised questions about giving further attention to clarifying the interrelationship among Christ, the church, the kingdom, and the world.

4. All presenters began with the Jesus of the Synoptic Gospels. While the assigned topics as well as Anabaptist tradition and practice may have made this starting point predictable, it also left some gaps. Many participants felt that the Old Testament, the Gospel of John, and the Epis-

tles should be given greater consideration in developing the themes of the consultation. Some participants felt that the resurrected Christ and the Holy Spirit were not given sufficient emphasis.

5. The focus on church as community was enthusiastically embraced as both biblical and Anabaptist in orientation. There was repeated concern however that we do not lose sight of the individual as an object of God's saving grace.

6. There was a call to continue working at defining both old and new terms more clearly (church, salvation, blessing, cross, atonement, convener, exclusiveness, pluralism, relativism).

7. A question not explicitly addressed but always present was: How do we read the Bible? Do we read it primarily for its stories or for its theological constructs? What interpretative approach enables us to read the text both as historical record and as guidance for faith and life? Can we be open to diverse perspectives and conceptual tensions in Scripture?

8. There were both strong reservations about and significant support for some tendencies among us to distance ourselves from the classical Christian creeds and their ontological implications. Even though most of the major presentations neither focused on nor addressed this issue in depth, it arose in several of the discussion and focus groups as well as in the final plenary session. Many participants expressed strong support for affirming the significance of the classical creeds for Christology in an Anabaptist and Mennonite perspective. Still others were not sure about the significance of this issue, that is, whether and why it should or should not be basic to Christology in a Mennonite perspective.

9. The respondents' (Daniel D. García Swartzentruber and Mary H. Schertz) contribution to the dialogue was noted with much appreciation. Both respondents suggested further considerations critical for our understanding of these issues. Participants requested that the respondents' papers be made accessible through publication or other means.

Finally, as a findings committee in keeping with what

we sensed as the spirit of the consultation, we suggest that we as Mennonite and Brethren in Christ churches can gain greater clarity about the theological concerns we have discussed both by 1) continuing the conversation begun at(Normal and by 2) seeking to be faithful churches in mission and discipleship under Jesus Christ our Lord in an ethically and religiously pluralistic world.

THE FINDINGS COMMITTEE: John Arthur Brubaker (Brethren in Christ), Tim Geddert (Mennonite Brethren), Lydia Harder (General Conference Mennonite Church), Elmer Jantzi (Conservative Mennonite Conference), Marlin E. Miller, chair (Mennonite Church), Robert J. Suderman (missionary, General Conference Mennonite Church).

Normal, Illinois
August 6, 1989

Bibliography

Barth, Markus. *Ephesians*, 2 vols. Doubleday, 1974.

Beachy, Alvin J. *The Concept of Grace in the Radical Reformation*. Nieuwkoop: B. de Graaf, 1977, 79-86; 178.

Bettenson, Henry, ed. *Documents of the Christian Church*, 2nd ed. London: Oxford, 1963.

Blough, Neal. *Christologie Anabaptiste. Pilgram Marpeck et l'humanité du Christ*. Genève: Labor et Fides, 1984.

Borg, Marcus. *Conflict, Holiness and Politics in the Teachings of Jesus*. Mellen, 1984.

Cullmann, Oscar. *The Christology of the New Testament*. Westminster, 1959.

De Jonge, Marinus, *Christology in Context*. Westminster, 1988.

Denck, Hans. "Whether God Is the Cause of Evil." *Spiritual and Anabaptist Writers*, ed. George H. Williams and Angel M. Mergal, 86-111. *Library of Christian Classics*, vol. 25. Philadelphia: Westminster, 1957.

Driver, John. *Understanding the Atonement for the Mission of the Church*. Scottdale/Kitchener: Herald Press, 1986.

Dunn, James D.G. *Christology in the Making*. Westminster, 1980.

Finger, Thomas N. *Christian Theology: An Eschatological Approach*. Nashville: Thomas Nelson Sons, 1985.

——. "The Way to Nicea: Reflections from a Mennonite Perspective." *Conrad Grebel Review* 3.3 (Fall 1985): 231-49. Also: *Journal of Ecumenical Studies* 24:2 (Spring 1987), 212-231.

Fuller, Reginald H. *The Foundations of New Testament Christology*. Scribners, 1965.

Gonzalez, Justo L. *A History of Christian Thought*. Vol. 1, *From the Beginnings to the Council of Chalcedon*. Nashville: Abingdon, 1970.

Hahn, Ferdinand. *Christologische Hoheitstitel*. Ruprecht, 1963.

Harvey, A.E. *Jesus and the Constraints of History*. Westminster, 1982.

Hauerwas, Stanley. *The Peaceable Kingdom: A Primer in Christian Ethics*. Notre Dame: University of Notre Dame Press, 1983.

——. *A Community of Character*. Notre Dame: University of Notre Dame Press, 1983.

——. *Christian Existence Today: Essays on Church, World and Living in Between*. Durham, North Carolina: The Labyrinth Press, 1988.

Hultgren, Arland J. *Christ and His Benefits*. Fortress, 1987.

Hurtado, Larry W. *One God, One Lord*. Fortress, 1988.

Jones, A. H. M. *Constantine and the Conversion of Europe*. New York: Macmillan, 1948; reprint, Toronto: University of Toronto, 1978.

Kaufman, Edmund G. *Basic Christian Convictions*. North Newton: Bethel College, 1972, 125-163.

Kaufman, Gordon D. *Systematic Theology: A Historicist Perspective*. New York: Charles Scribner's Sons, 1978.

Keeney, William E. *The Development of Dutch Anabaptist Thought and Practice from 1539-1564*. Nieuwkoop: B. de Graaf, 1968, 89-113; 191- 221.

——. "The Incarnation: A Central Theological Concept," *A Legacy of Faith*, C. J. Dyck, ed. Newton: Faith and Life, 1962, 55-68.

Klaassen, Walter. *Anabaptism in Outline*. Kitchener/ Scottdale: Herald Press, 1981, 23-40. Excerpts from sixteenth century Anabaptists and Mennonites in English translation.

——. *Anabaptism: Neither Catholic nor Protestant*. Waterloo, Ont.: Conrad Press, 1973.

Knitter, Paul. *No Other Name?* Maryknoll: Orbis Books, 1985.

Kraus, C. Norman. *Jesus Christ our Lord. Christology from a Disciple's Perspective.* Scottdale/Kitchener: Herald, 1987.

Leith, John H., editor. *Creeds of the Churches: A Reader in Christian Doctrine from the Bible to the Present.* Atlanta: John Knox Press, 1977. Confessional and creedal statements from the New Testament to contemporary Protestant and Roman Catholic declarations, including Anabaptist and Mennonite confessions of Schleitheim and Dordrecht.

Lindbeck, George A. *The Nature of Doctrine.* Westminster, 1984.

Loewen, Howard John. *One Lord, One Church, One Hope, and One God: Mennonite Confessions of Faith.* Institute of Mennonite Studies, 1985. An anthology of Mennonite confessional statements from the sixteenth to the late twentieth century.

Lohfink, Gerhard. *Jesus and Community.* Philadelphia: Fortress, 1984.

Lohse, Bernhard. *A Short History of Christian Doctrine.* Translated by F. Ernest Stoeffler. Philadelphia: Fortress, 1966.

MacIntyre, Alasdair. *After Virtue: A Study in Moral Theory.* (Second Edition) Notre Dame: University of Notre Dame Press, 1984.

——. *Whose Justice? Which Rationality?* Notre Dame: University of Notre Dame Press, 1988.

MacMullen, Ramsay. *Constantine.* Dial Press, 1969; reprint, London: Croom Helm, 1987.

Marpeck, Pilgram. *The Writings of Pilgram Marpeck.* William Klassen and Walter Klaassen, eds. and trans. Classics of the Radical Reformation, vol. 3. Kitchener/Scottdale: Herald Press, 1978.

McClendon, James W., Jr. *Ethics: Systematic Theology.* (Volume I), Nashville: Abingdon, 1986.

Menno Simons. *The Complete Writings of Menno Simons, c.1496-1561.* Leonard Verduin, trans. John C. Wenger, ed. Scottdale: Herald Press, 1956.

Meyer, B.F. *The Aims of Jesus.* London: SCM, 1979.

Miller, Marlin E. "Christological Concepts of the Classical Creeds and Mennonite Confessions of Faith" *AMBS*

Bulletin, 52 (May 1989), 7-11.

——. "Christology." To be published in *Mennonite Encyclopedia*, vol. 5. Scottdale: Herald Press.

Moltmann, Jurgen. *The Crucified God: The Cross of Christ as the Foundation and Criticism of Christian Theology.* London: SCM Press, 1974.

Morris, Leon. *The Atonement.* InterVarsity, 1983.

Moule, C.F.D. *The Origins of Christology.* Cambridge University Press, 1977.

Neill, Stephen. *The Supremacy of Jesus.* Downers Grove: Intervarsity, 1984.

Newbigin, Lesslie. *The Open Secret.* Grand Rapids: Eerdmans, 1978.

O'Collins, Gerald, S.J. *What Are They Saying About Jesus?* Mahwah, N.J.: Paulist Press, 1982.

Ollenburger, Ben. "Christology and Creeds," *AMBS Bulletin*, 52 (May 1989), 1-3.

Pelikan, Jaroslav. *The Christian Tradition: A History of the Development of Doctrine.* Vol. 1, *The Emergence of the Catholic Tradition (100-600).* Chicago: University of Chicago, 1971.

Richard, Earl. *Jesus: One and Many.* Michael Glazier, 1988.

Richardson, Alan. *Creeds in the Making: A Short Introduction to the History of Christian Doctrine.* Reprint, Philadelphia: Fortress, 1981.

Richardson, Cyril C. *The Doctrine of the Trinity.* New York: Abingdon, 1958.

Riches, John. *Jesus and the Transformation of Judaism.* Seabury, 1982.

Sanders, E.P. *Jesus and Judaism.* Fortress, 1985.

Scriven, Charles. *The Transformation of Culture: Christian Social Ethics After H. Richard Niebuhr.* Scottdale: Herald Press, 1988.

Seeberg, Reinhold. *Text-Book of the History of Doctrines.* Charles E. Hay, trans. Grand Rapids: Baker Book House, 1961.

Stroup, George W. "Chalcedon Revisited." *Theology Today* 35.2 (April 1978): 52-64.

Toews, John E. *Romans*, to be published, Believers Church Commentary Series, Herald Press.

——. "The Nature of the Church," Mennonite Brethren
Study Conference, Normal, Illinois, August 2-4, 1989.
Visser't Hooft, W. A. *No Other Name.* London: SCM, 1963.
Weaver, J. Denny. "A Believer's Church Christology."
Mennonite Quarterly Review 57.2 (April 1983): 112-131.
——. *Becoming Anabaptist: The Origin and Significance
of Sixteenth-Century Anabaptism.* Scottdale/Kitchener:
Herald Press, 1987.
——. "The Work of Christ: On the Difficulty of Identifying
an Anabaptist Perspective." *Mennonite Quarterly
Review* 59.2 (April 1985): 107-129.
Wenger, John Christian. *Introduction to Theology.*
Scottdale: Herald Press, 1954. 62-70; 193-211; 334-359.
Walter Wink. *Violence and Nonviolence in South Africa:
Jesus's Third Way.* Philadelphia: New Society, 1987.
Yoder, John Howard. *The Politics of Jesus.* Grand Rapids:
Eerdmans, 1972.
——. *Preface to Theology: Christology and Theological
Method.* Elkhart: Goshen Biblical Seminary; distribut-
ed by Mennonite Cooperative Bookstore.
——. *The Priestly Kingdom: Social Ethics as Gospel.* Notre
Dame: University of Notre Dame Press, 1984.

Indexes

discipline 40
discipling and disciplining church 54
divorce 67, 81
Driver, John 30, 33, 48

Easter people 81
ecclesia 38
ecclesiology 121, 124; believers' church 103; concern of Christology 53; Mennonite 54
Ediger, Jerry v
empire, as bearer of God's providence 95
enemies, treatment of 59
epistemology 65
Epistles 62, 124, 126
ethical discernment 39, 40
ethical inquiry, conceptual language needed 76; nature of 74
ethics 93, 121, 124; aimed at justice 66; and discipleship 56; as communal 63; as gift 63; as historical analysis 67; as identity 67; as private 62; becoming God's people 68; being like Jesus 62; communal functions 67; decision making 67; dualistic 69; emperor as norm 95; for formation 63; healing relationships 67; in story language 75; interpreting issues 67; Jesus as normative 34, 75, 98; Jesus irrelevant for 57; learning morality 65; narrative approach 75; never unqualified 63; relevance of Jesus 69; role of Jesus and church 57; traditional approaches 74
Eve 51
evil, power of 61
exclusiveness 3, 127; God's grace manifested 30; God's responsibility for 22; in Christ and not in community 32; New Testament evidence 30; non-transferable 20; not responsible to defend 31; of Hispanic culture 25; of institutional church 25; of the market order 29; of the preacher 27; scandal of 19, 23; unsupported by coercion 31
exclusivism 19
expiation 44

faith 18, 81, 122; emperor as norm, 95
fall 5
feminism v; and maleness of Jesus 125
fides ex auditus 65
finality and finitude, tensions of 32
Finger, Thomas iv, v, 106-114, 115, 141
followers of Jesus, as people of God 68
forgiveness 40, 44, 58, 62, 71
Freytag, Walter 31
fundamentalism 1, 24, 29

Geddert, Tim v, 128
General Conference Mennonite Church iii, 107, 128
Gentiles, access through Christ 45; equal partners with Jews 46; people of God 46; sins of 45
God, acts in history 18; and historical process 19; as judge 71; as moral authority for ethics 63; as Savior 72; as sufferer 69; call of 71; inactivity of 45; knowing through Christ v; model of righteousness 45; providence of 118; righteousness 44, 46; sovereignty of 14; Spirit of 19
God's love, as invitation 71
God's truth, invitational nature of 71
Good Samaritan 66, 79
Gospels 37, 43, 62; favored by Anabaptists 99; Synoptic 110, 124, 126
grace 13, 71, 127
Gregory Nazianzus 86
Gregory of Nyssa 86
Grimsrud, Ted v
Gutierrez, Gustavo 27

Hades, gates of 39
Harder, Lydia v, 128
Hauerwas, Stanley 63
Hayek, Friedrich 28
healing 41; restoration of God's people 41
Heim, Karl 31
heterosexuals 71
Hispanic conquest and colonization 24
historical Jesus debate 57

Luke, Gospel of 58; new life in
Christ 82; proclamation theme 77
Luke/Acts, use of "must" 15
Luther, Martin 100, 101

Machpelah, cave of 51
Marpeck, Pilgram 100, 101, 109
Mary 101; song of 58
Menno Simons 101, 109; Christology nonstandard 101
Mennonite Brethren Church iii, 107, 128
Mennonite Central Committee 76
Mennonite Church iii, 107, 128
Mennonite confessions 36
Mennonite World Conference iii, 107, 120
Mennonites, seeing Christ and church related 34
Messiah 50, 60, 90
Metz, J. 27
Miller, Marlin E. v, 128
mission iii, 120, 122, 126; Anabaptist example 32; apostolic self-understanding 21; as building the church 54; Christology's meaning 17; dialogic style 22; dialogue iii; faithful practice 21; irenic strategies 123; irenic style 22; mediatorial stance 21; message and messenger 20; messenger and witness 21; nonjudgmental attitudes 123; participation in suffering 32; peace as way 22, 31; peaceful cooperation 29; significance of Christ 126; suggestions for 31; theology of 121; truthful perspectives 18
Missionary Conference, Jerusalem 1928 29
Moltmann, Jurgen 27
monotheism 13, 18, 86, 89
Moses 51, 52, 80
mysticism 99
narrative ethics 78
New Testament, Christological reflection 37
Nicaragua 76
Nicea 56, 85, 86, 92, 94, 97, 109, 112
Nicene Creed 85, 98, 107, 108, 109, 110
nonresistance 100
normativity 71
Novak, Michael 28

obedience 125
Old Testament 126
ontology 36, 85, 110
Origen 112
orthodoxy 118

parables, Christological claim 9
Passover 43
Paul 17, 43, 50; reconciliation language 46; righteousness language 45; theology of 52
peace 22
people of God, as followers of Jesus 68; images for 41
peoplehood 50; created by Christ 43; created by suffering 43; New Testament concern 53; titles of Christ 51
pluralism 3, 4, 5, 31, 127
pollution 47
poor 58
poverty 66
power 20, 47, 61
prayer 41
predestination 100
Preheim, Vern iv
process philosophy 4
proclamation, evangelistic v; gospel theme 77; obligation to 16
Prodigal Son 79
Protestant evangelization 26
Protestantism 26

reconciliation 46; new creation 46; to create peoplehood 46
redemption 44, 46; theology of 18
Reesor, Rachel Helen v
Reimer, A. James v
relativism 3, 4, 20, 24, 28, 29, 31, 127
religion, as rebellion 31; as thirst for God 31; demonic forces within 31; Indian 25; phenomenology of 29
repentance 11, 12, 40
resurrection 13, 48, 93, 113, 124, 127 and nonviolence of Jesus 80; as ethical basis 80; as transforming power 81; linked to cross 80, 82
revelation 68, 123; general 19; special 19
revolution, moral 73
righteousness 11, 20, 45
rock 42, 49, 53; as image in

138

Judaism 38
Roman Catholic Church 25, 26, 124
Rosenkranz, Gerhard 31
rule of God 42
Ruth 80
Rycroft, W. Stanley 26

salvation 11, 13, 14, 15, 16, 17, 18,
20, 23, 25, 27, 30, 58, 71, 72, 81,
108, 109, 113, 122, 124, 125, 127;
and the church 123; basic paradigm 11; communal nature of 115;
corporate dimension 123; final 15;
history 11, 16; not apart from
church 54; offered to world 52
Satan 39, 51
Schertz, Mary H. iv, 74-78, 79, 127,
141
Schipani, Daniel v
sectarianism 26
secularism 29
Segundo, J. L. 27, 28
Sermon on the Mount 9, 58, 61
Servant Songs 43
servanthood 10, 62, 67, 109
Seth 51
sexism 66
Shafer, Don iv
shalom 60
Shelly, Patricia v
shekina 49
Shem 51
Shenk, Wilbert, v
Sider, E. Morris v
sin 5, 44, 51, 52, 59, 60, 62, 70,
power of 47
slavery 46, 47
Son of God 50, 52, 60, 91, 92
Son of Man 50
sonship 12
Spain 24
spirituality 68, 125
story, power of 76
Strasbourg Missions Consultation
120
Study Conference on Christology
107; findings 120; purpose 120
Suderman, Robert J. v, 128
Swartzentruber, Daniel D. García
iv, 24-32, 127, 141
sword, way of 68
syncretism 19

Tertullian 112

theology, of covenant peoplehood 44
Toews, John E. iv, 33-55, 76, 113,
119, 121, 123, 124, 126, 141
tolerance 3, 19
transubstantiation 25
Trinitarianism v
Trinity 86, 92, 100
Triumphalism 123
truth 23, 66, 123, exclusive dimension 23; search for 5

ugly ditch 19
*Understanding the Atonement for
the Mission of the Church* 33
unity 4
Utopia 28

violence 60, 69, 70, justification of
80; temptation to 25
voluntarism 3

Waltner, Erland iii-v, 141
Weaver, Dorothy Jean v
Weaver, J. Denny iv, 83-105, 106,
115-119, 121, 141
Wink, Walter 61
wisdom 16
Word 92, 100, 109
world 126
worship 67, 68, 75, 125

Yahweh, lordship of 50
Yoder, John Howard 34, 56, 62

Zechariah, song of 58

Scripture index

Hebrew Scriptures

Genesis
6 51
28 38

Exodus 46
4:22 91

Psalms
2:7 91

Isaiah 43
2:2-4 38
42:14 45

139

The Writers

George Brunk III is dean of Eastern Mennonite Seminary, Harrisonburg, Virginia.

Daniel D. García Swartzentruber is professor of church history at the Buenos Aires Biblical Institute and visiting professor of church history at the Protestant School of Theology in Buenos Aires.

John E. Toews is dean of Mennonite Brethren Biblical Seminary, Fresno, California.

Harry Huebner is associate professor of philosophy and theology at Canadian Mennonite Bible College, Winnipeg.

Mary H. Schertz is assistant professor of New Testament at Goshen Biblical Seminary, Elkhart, Indiana.

J. Denny Weaver is professor of religion, Bluffton College, Bluffton, Ohio.

Thomas Finger is visiting professor of theology at Eastern Mennonite Seminary, Harrisonburg, Virginia.

Erland Waltner is past president of Mennonite Biblical Seminary, Elkhart, Indiana, and former professor of English Bible.